SELLING WITH INTENT

Leaving Nothing to Chance

By

Rick Cochran

SELLING WITH INTENT

Printed In United States of America
Published by: USA Publishing Hub

Dedication

This book is a culmination of years of experiences, lessons, and unwavering support from many remarkable individuals who have been a part of my journey. It would not have been possible without their guidance, encouragement, and inspiration.

To my children—Monica, Alexandra, Richard, Alexa, and Isabel—thank you for reminding me of the importance of perseverance and passion.

To my parents, Dick and DeeDee, whose wisdom and unwavering belief and support in my potential instilled in me the confidence to chase my dreams. Your timeless advice to "always give my best" has been my guiding principle throughout this journey.

To my father-in-law, whose challenge to "talk to me when you publish" became a rallying cry that propelled me to turn an idea into reality.

And most importantly, to my wife Lori,—my unwavering supporter, my sounding board, and my greatest partner in life. Your encouragement, patience, and belief in me, even on days when I doubted myself, gave me the strength to keep writing. This book is as much yours as it is mine.

Finally, to every reader who picks up this book, thank you for allowing me to share my journey and insights with you. My hope is that it inspires, informs, and motivates you to achieve your own extraordinary goals. This book was written with intent, and it is my honor to now share it with the world.

With deepest gratitude,

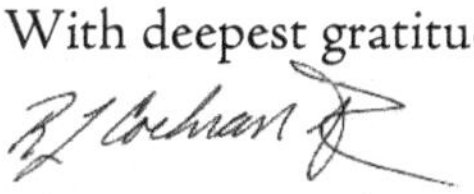

Richard L. Cochran Jr

Table of Contents

Using This Book: This book has been designed to serve as both a comprehensive guide and a practical reference for sales leaders at every stage of their career. Each chapter focuses on a specific aspect of sales leadership, breaking down complex concepts into actionable insights. The format allows you to read sequentially for a full understanding or navigate directly to the sections most relevant to your current challenges. Chapter overviews provide quick summaries to help you pinpoint key topics, while detailed subtopics ensure no aspect of the sales leadership journey is overlooked.

Chapter 1

Understanding the Role of Sales Leaders

Overview: This chapter introduces the critical role of sales leaders in driving business success. It explores the core responsibilities of sales leaders, common challenges they face, and the evolving nature of sales leadership in the digital age.

1. The Importance of Sales Leadership
2. Key Responsibilities of Sales Leaders
3. Common Challenges Faced by Sales Leader
4. The Evolving Role of Sales Leaders
5. The Critical Role of CRM Proficiency
6. Case Study: Omega Financial's Leadership Evolution

Chapter 2

Developing a Winning Sales Strategy

Overview: This chapter provides actionable insights into creating a successful sales strategy. It covers leveraging AI tools, conducting SWOT analysis, and tracking sales performance for maximum efficiency.

1. Integrating AI Tools for Strategy
2. Strategic Planning with SWOT Analysis
3. Tracking Performance and Engagement

Chapter 3

Building and Managing a High-Performing Sales Team

Overview: This chapter focuses on assembling and managing an exceptional sales team. Topics include strategic recruitment, performance management, continuous training, and fostering a high-performance culture.

1. Strategic Recruitment
2. Performance Management Software Integration
3. Continuous Training and Development
4. Data-Driven Decision Making
5. Cultivating a High-Performance Culture

Chapter 4

Implementing Effective Sales Techniques

Overview: Discover a wide array of proven sales techniques, from consultative selling to digital and behavioral approaches. This chapter provides tools to refine your sales tactics for better outcomes.

1. Consultative Selling
2. Solution Selling
3. Upselling and Cross-Selling
4. Inbound and Outbound Selling
5. SPIN and Challenger Selling
6. Social and Behavioral Selling
7. Value-Based and Referral Selling
8. Storytelling and Direct Selling
9. Transactional Selling

Chapter 5

Overcoming Sales Objections and Closing Deals

Overview: Handling objections and closing deals are pivotal sales skills. This chapter delves into objection-handling strategies and advanced closing techniques to secure sales confidently.

1. The Nature of Sales Objections
2. Overcoming Price Objections
3. Addressing Feature Objections
4. Handling Competitor Comparisons
5. Advanced Negotiation Techniques
6. Using the "Feel, Felt, Found" Method
7. Effective Closing Techniques

Chapter 6

Measuring Sales Success and Driving Continuous Improvement

Overview: Explore methods for measuring sales success and ensuring continuous improvement. This chapter highlights the use of KPIs, feedback loops, and process improvement strategies.

1. Role of Data Visualization
2. Continuous Process Improvement
3. Tools for Measuring Success
4. Key Performance Indicators (KPIs)
5. Effective Performance Reviews
6. Implementing Feedback Loops

Chapter 7

Staying Ahead of the Competition

Overview: Staying competitive requires strategic insights and agility. This chapter examines tools like Porter's Five Forces and methods for monitoring competitors and adapting to market trends.

1. Porter's Five Forces
2. Analyzing and Monitoring Competitors
3. Developing Unique Selling Propositions
4. Adapting to Market Changes and Trends

Chapter 8

The Future of Sales Leadership

Overview: Sales leadership is evolving with emerging technologies and ethical practices. This chapter discusses machine learning, AI, blockchain, and corporate social responsibility (CSR).

1. Emerging Technologies
2. Ethical Selling and Corporate Social Responsibility
3. Developing Future-Ready Strategies

Chapter 9

Embracing Change and Using Stress to Promote Growth

Overview: Change and stress can catalyze growth. This chapter explores strategies for transforming resistance into innovation and fostering resilience in sales teams.

1. The Role of Change in Growth
2. Transforming Stress into Innovation
3. Building Resilience and Adaptability

About the Author

Rick Cochran – Visionary Leader, Innovator, and Mentor

Rick Cochran is a dynamic leader whose career spans startups, Fortune 50 corporations, turnarounds, spinouts, and consulting across multiple industries, including healthcare, technology, education, waste management, and manufacturing He has consistently led transformative initiatives by integrating data, technology, processes, and people to deliver innovative solutions that enhance business performance, uncover new revenue streams, and elevate the overall experience for both customers and employees.

With leadership roles at Thomson Reuters, Electronic Data Systems (EDS), Perot Systems/Dell, Herff Jones, Jostens Corporation, and Browning-Ferris Industries, Rick has pioneered advancements in operational efficiency, workforce development, and sales strategy. He has worked extensively in education, healthcare, and enterprise technology, leveraging his expertise to align business objectives with human-centered innovation.

Innovator in Healthcare & Workforce Development

Dedicated to advancing healthcare solutions, Rick has led groundbreaking initiatives such as a state-of-the-art learning portal and HMG-U, a nonprofit educational organization. These programs, along with his work at HMG Healthcare, LaVie Care Centers, and Premier Healthcare, leverage Generative AI and strategic process optimization to enhance workforce training, improve patient outcomes, and transform healthcare delivery.

As the founder and board member of ExSells, CollegeChoiceToday and SkillCare Connect, Rick has developed AI-powered career counseling and workforce development platforms, impacting thousands of professionals. His contributions to education and business have been recognized by leaders such as Chairman and Commissioner of the Texas Workforce commission, Bryan Daniel, Texas State Senator Brian Birdwell, Texas Governor Greg Abbott, and Presidential Candidate Ross Perot.

Leadership in Education & Technology

Rick has been instrumental in shaping education and career pathways by forging strategic partnerships with institutions such as Biola University, Baylor University, the University of Texas, the University of Maryland Global Campus, and Career Education Corporation. As a board member and founder of HMG-U and SkillCare Connect, he has developed innovative programs that integrate online learning, classroom instruction, and hands-on training. His efforts have earned recognition from the Texas Workforce Commission for advancing workforce development and bridging critical skill gaps.

Beyond higher education, Rick has worked on nationally recognized programs, including launching the Congressional Medal of Honor Foundation's character education initiative while at Jostens and collaborating with Hulman & Company (parent of the Indianapolis 500) on STEM-focused learning programs.

Entrepreneur, Mentor & Strategic Consultant

In the technology sector, Rick mentors' entrepreneurs through the Austin Technology Council and the University of Texas Venture Mentoring Services, a program modeled after MIT's approach to guiding startups. He also co-founded the Office of Human Capital Management and Development at the University of Maryland Global Campus, where he designed specialized educational solutions for military and intelligence professionals.

His work in healthcare technology includes developing the first HIPAA-compliant electronic data interchange (EDI) in collaboration with a Ross Perot-led company, transforming health claims processing for multiple Blue Cross Blue Shield affiliates.

Following the September 11 attacks, Rick and team partnered with NYC Fire Commissioner Thomas Von Essen to create a centralized database for fire suppression best practices, demonstrating his ability to build systems that prioritize both innovation and human impact.

Recognized Thought Leader & Author

With firsthand experience in sales, operations, and leadership, Rick brings real-world insights gained from navigating turnarounds, launching startups, and driving strategic growth. His deep understanding of these challenges has made him a sought-after advisor across corporate and nonprofit sectors. As a guest lecturer, mentor, and board member, he shares practical, experience-based knowledge that empowers professionals to achieve measurable success.

In 2025, Rick released *Selling with Intent: Leaving Nothing to Chance*, a book that distills his decades of experience into actionable strategies for sales professionals. By aligning data, technology, and human connection, his work continues to inspire professionals to achieve meaningful, results-driven success.

Rick holds multiple patents and remains committed to pushing the boundaries of innovation, leadership, and workforce transformation.

Foreword

Selling with Intent - A Champion's Perspective on Sales

In a world saturated with sales advice and fleeting trends, Rick Cochran offers a refreshing and transformative approach to the art of selling. *Selling with Intent* is not just another sales manual—it's a masterclass in building authentic connections, achieving meaningful results, and excelling amid the ever-evolving challenges of the sales profession.

Rick's career is as remarkable as it is diverse. From closing $800 million deals across industries like healthcare, technology, and education to selling everyday products like pots, pans, and trash containers, Rick has honed the art of sales at every level. His adaptability, deep understanding of human connections, and results-driven mindset have distinguished him as a true sales professional.

A natural competitor, Rick's drive for excellence was instilled early in life. As a linebacker at the University of Miami, he played a role in securing the school's first national championship. This same competitive spirit and discipline have defined his career, fueling his success in both sales and leadership roles across a range of industries.

Rick has collaborated with some of the most influential figures in business and politics, from local leaders to federal policymakers. His ability to work with high-level decision-makers has shaped transformative initiatives in sectors like healthcare and education. Whether negotiating multimillion-dollar contracts or contributing to groundbreaking policies, Rick's expertise has left a lasting impact.

Rick's journey also reflects the challenges of balancing a demanding career with personal values. As a dedicated father and professional, he understands the complexities of achieving success while staying grounded. *Selling with Intent* distills his decades of experience into actionable strategies for professionals at every stage of their sales journey.

Are you ready to elevate your sales game? With lessons shaped on the football field, refined in the boardroom, and proven across diverse industries, Rick's story will inspire you to sell smarter, foster stronger relationships, and achieve enduring success—all with intent. Dive into *Selling with Intent* and unlock the champion within you.

Introduction

Simplicity in Sales, a Proven Path to Results

In over thirty years of navigating the intricate landscape of sales and management, Rick Cochran has gained profound insights and crafted actionable strategies that transcend industries. This book distills these lessons into an indispensable guide for sales leaders seeking to enhance their acumen and drive impactful results.

Rick highlights a critical issue in sales education: 90% of training resources fail to create meaningful change, leaving only 10% capable of delivering transformative insights. This book challenges sales professionals to move beyond superficial practices and embrace proven methods that genuinely elevate team performance.

More than just a sales manual, this guide serves as a manifesto advocating for the power of simplicity and effectiveness in sales strategies. Rick's career has revealed that the most successful salespeople develop straightforward, effective habits that streamline their approach and yield maximum results.

Think of your most challenging sales situation—whether it involved technical complexity, emotional intensity, or both. These scenarios demand sophisticated yet deliberate strategies. Despite their variety, these challenges share underlying patterns that this book unpacks for your benefit.

Rick's journey spans multiple industries. In every role, his focus was on driving revenue while continuously learning, adapting, and applying insights across sectors.

The genesis of this book stems from Rick's personal collection of lessons and strategies, refined into a comprehensive resource through the encouragement of colleagues and industry experts. It is not merely a manual for aspiring sales leaders; it is a testament to the transformative power of simplicity in achieving sales excellence.

Welcome to *Selling with Intent* — a transformative tool authored by a seasoned expert whose battle-tested strategies and insights will guide you to mastery and success in the dynamic world of sales.

Rick's journey spans multiple industries, and in every role, his focus has been on driving revenue while ensuring that growth is matched by the development of strong internal infrastructure to support it. He is committed to continuously learning, adapting, and applying insights across diverse sectors to fuel sustainable success.

CHAPTER 1

The Beating Heart of Your Business—Sales Leadership

Your role as a sales leader is to set your team up to win.

– Tom Abbott

As the leader of your sales team, you embody the beating heart that keeps your business alive and thriving. Your role is the vital force that pumps energy, direction, and purpose through every vein of the organization. Without a strong, visionary sales leader, a business is like a lifeless body, devoid of the lifeblood needed to grow, evolve, and succeed in a competitive marketplace.

This is no ordinary job; it is a calling. As a sales leader, you wear many hats. You are equal parts strategist, motivator, coach, and trailblazer. Your responsibilities encompass defining the sales vision, creating a roadmap, and inspiring your team to bring it to fruition. Daily, you juggle forecasting, training, problem-solving, and finding innovative ways to help your team close deals and nurture customer relationships.

Your role requires a unique blend of quantitative and qualitative skills, combining hard data analytics with emotional intelligence. You must seamlessly merge the analytical mind of a data scientist with the intuitive touch of a psychologist. Through this synthesis, you provide your team with the tools, knowledge, and support needed to realize their potential.

Above all, a sales leader is a relentless student of the craft. The sales landscape is in constant flux, shaped by new technologies, evolving buyer behaviors, and an unending wave of competitive challenges. Mastering this role demands perpetual learning, adaptation, and refinement to ensure your team remains agile, innovative, and ahead of the curve.

In the following pages, we will delve into the core competencies, strategies, and mindsets that define the most successful sales leaders. Prepare to become the vital heartbeat propelling your organization to new heights of growth and success. The future of your business depends on it. Let's begin with the importance of sales leadership.

The Importance of Sales Leadership

As the captain steering the sales ship, your role is central to your business's success, resilience, and long-term viability. Without strong, strategic sales leadership, even the most talented sales team can falter, failing to reach its full potential or deliver the results your organization needs to thrive in a competitive marketplace.

Transforming Talent into a Unified Force

Great sales leadership goes beyond managing individuals—it transforms a group of talented sellers into a cohesive, high-performing team. You are the guiding force that aligns your team around a shared vision, cultivating a sense of purpose, motivation, and ownership of the company's growth objectives. Effective leaders inspire trust and foster an environment where sellers feel valued, supported, and equipped to excel. With strong leadership, teams don't just hit quotas—they exceed them, driving sustainable growth.

Empowering Through Vision and Support

Leadership is not just about setting ambitious targets; it's about empowering your team to achieve them. By clearly communicating the organization's vision and providing the resources, training, and tools necessary for success, you build a foundation of confidence and competence within your team. Whether it's leveraging technology, refining processes, or investing in professional development, effective sales leaders ensure their team has everything required to thrive.

Consequences of Poor Sales Leadership

The absence of strong sales leadership can have devastating consequences. Without clear direction, teams become disjointed, relying on inconsistent individual efforts to navigate an increasingly complex sales landscape. This can lead to erratic performance, missed opportunities, and a negative customer experience. Moreover, the lack of leadership often results in demoralized teams, higher turnover rates, and eroded trust within the organization—a ripple effect that impacts the entire business.

The Multifaceted Role of a Sales Leader

Sales leadership is not a single-dimensional role; it encompasses various interconnected responsibilities:

1. **Strategist:** Craft the roadmap that guides the team toward ambitious yet attainable goals.
2. **Mentor:** Invest in the personal and professional development of your team members through tailored coaching and constructive feedback.
3. **Problem-Solver:** Anticipate challenges and proactively remove obstacles that hinder progress.
4. **Visionary:** Inspire innovation and creativity, fostering a culture that embraces change and seeks continuous improvement.
5. **Customer Advocate:** Represent the voice of the customer within the organization, ensuring that strategies align with customer needs and market dynamics.

Leadership Beyond Numbers

While sales results are critical, impactful leadership extends beyond metrics. Exceptional leaders create a culture of accountability, recognition, and mutual respect. Celebrating successes, learning from setbacks, and maintaining an open line of communication strengthens team morale and commitment. They also foster an environment where innovation is encouraged, ensuring team members feel confident proposing fresh ideas and solutions.

Emotional Intelligence and Empathy

An often-overlooked but vital aspect of sales leadership is emotional intelligence. The ability to understand and manage your own emotions while recognizing and influencing the emotions of others can significantly enhance team dynamics. Empathetic leaders build stronger relationships, navigate conflicts effectively, and create a supportive atmosphere where team members feel heard and valued.

Leveraging Diversity and Inclusion

Diverse teams bring a wealth of perspectives, experiences, and ideas that drive creativity and innovation. As a sales leader, fostering an inclusive culture ensures every team member feels respected and empowered to contribute. This not only strengthens team cohesion but also enhances problem-solving and decision-making capabilities, leading to improved performance.

Adapting to a Changing Landscape

In today's fast-evolving sales environment, leaders must embrace change and lead by example. Staying ahead means adopting emerging technologies, like AI-driven analytics and CRM tools, to enhance decision-making and productivity. It also involves understanding shifts in buyer behavior and guiding the team to adapt to new customer expectations, such as personalized engagement and omnichannel communication.

Sales leaders must also prepare their teams for macroeconomic shifts, such as fluctuating markets or industry disruptions. Resilience and adaptability are essential traits, allowing the sales function to pivot strategies effectively without losing momentum.

Long-Term Impact of Effective Leadership

When done right, the effects of great sales leadership extend far beyond quarterly reports. Higher win rates, stronger customer relationships, a motivated and innovative team, and accelerated revenue growth are just the beginning. Effective leadership creates a legacy of excellence, setting the stage for future success and ensuring the organization's long-term health and competitiveness.

Moreover, successful sales leaders build a pipeline of future leaders within their teams. By mentoring and developing high-potential talent, they create a sustainable leadership model that ensures the organization's growth and resilience for years to come.

By embracing the multifaceted nature of this role, sales leaders can elevate their teams and organizations to unparalleled levels of success. In the hands of a capable leader, the sales function becomes a powerhouse of growth, resilience, and innovation.

The Key Responsibilities of a Sales Leader

Crafting the Sales Strategy

Defining the sales strategy is at the heart of your role. This roadmap guides your team toward achieving growth objectives by blending market analysis, customer insights, competitive intelligence, and a deep understanding of your unique value proposition. It's your job to chart the course, set ambitious yet attainable targets, and align every activity, process, and investment with the overarching vision.

Developing and Coaching Your Team

Your sales team is your most valuable asset. Cultivating their skills, motivation, and success is essential. This involves comprehensive training, personalized coaching, and opportunities for professional development. By identifying each team member's strengths, growth areas, and career aspirations, you can tailor your approach to help them achieve new heights of excellence.

Driving Sales Execution

A well-crafted strategy is meaningless without flawless execution. Your role involves tracking pipeline activity, analyzing performance metrics, and resolving bottlenecks swiftly. Collaborate with your team to refine processes, sharpen messaging, and implement tools and technologies that enhance productivity and efficiency.

Fostering a High-Performance Culture

Sustainable success is about more than numbers. You must nurture a dynamic, high-energy culture where your team feels empowered and passionate about their work. Celebrate wins, provide constructive feedback, and model the behaviors and mindsets you want to see throughout the organization.

Serving as the Voice of the Customer

You hold a unique position to understand your customers' needs, pain points, and evolving behaviors. Leverage this insight to act as a bridge between your sales team and the broader organization, ensuring customer intelligence shapes product development, marketing, and strategy.

Future Trends in Sales Leadership

AI-Driven Insights

Artificial Intelligence (AI) is revolutionizing sales by providing predictive analytics, customer behavior insights, and lead scoring. Sales leaders can harness AI tools to identify high-value prospects, tailor messaging, and forecast sales outcomes with precision. The ability to leverage AI effectively will become a defining trait of successful sales organizations.

Virtual and Hybrid Selling

The rise of remote work and digital-first buyer preferences has solidified virtual selling as a standard practice. Sales leaders must equip their teams with skills to thrive in virtual environments, including mastering video conferencing platforms, building rapport online, and leveraging digital tools to simulate face-to-face engagement.

Omnichannel Strategies

Modern buyers expect seamless interactions across multiple channels—from social media to in-person meetings. Sales leaders need to design and implement omnichannel strategies that integrate digital and traditional approaches. This includes using CRM systems to unify customer interactions and deliver consistent experiences.

Ethical and Sustainable Selling

As consumers and businesses become more values-driven, sales leaders must emphasize ethical practices and sustainability in their strategies. Transparent communication, responsible product offerings, and commitment to social and environmental causes will be critical for building trust and long-term relationships.

Upskilling for Digital Literacy

Continuous learning and skill development are essential in a rapidly evolving sales landscape. Sales leaders must invest in training programs that enhance digital literacy, including data analytics, CRM mastery, and proficiency with emerging technologies like augmented reality (AR) and virtual reality (VR).

Emphasis on Soft Skills

While technology enhances efficiency, the importance of soft skills like empathy, active listening, and adaptability remains paramount. Sales leaders must balance technological advancements with human connection to build trust and foster deeper relationships with customers.

Integration of AI-Enhanced Coaching

AI tools are also being used to analyze sales calls, identify coaching opportunities, and provide real-time feedback. This technology empowers sales leaders to offer personalized coaching that addresses individual team member needs, ultimately boosting performance and job satisfaction.

Data Privacy and Compliance

As data becomes central to sales strategies, adhering to privacy regulations like GDPR and CCPA is critical. Sales leaders must ensure their teams are trained in ethical data usage and compliance to maintain customer trust and avoid legal repercussions.

Case Study: Omega Financial's Digital Transformation

Omega Financial, a leader in wealth management, faced significant challenges that impeded their ability to deliver optimal results. Key pain points included fragmented data across multiple platforms, inefficient processes that drained productivity, and a lack of centralized customer insights. Recognizing the need for a transformative solution,

Omega Financial implemented Kylas CRM to streamline operations and enhance team performance.

Challenges

1. **Data Fragmentation:** Sales and customer data were stored across disconnected spreadsheets and systems, leading to inefficiencies in accessing critical information.
2. **Inefficient Workflows:** Manual processes slowed down operations, increasing errors and reducing the team's ability to focus on strategic tasks.
3. **Limited Collaboration:** The absence of a unified platform hindered effective communication and collaboration among team members.

Solutions Implemented with Kylas CRM

- **Centralized Customer Data:** Kylas CRM provided a single source of truth for all customer interactions, consolidating data and enabling better decision-making.
- **Workflow Automation:** Automating repetitive tasks, such as follow-ups and data entry, freed up time for high-value activities and reduced errors.
- **Enhanced Collaboration Tools:** The platform's team dashboards and real-time updates improved communication and alignment across the sales organization.
- **Insightful Reporting and Analytics:** Customizable reports gave Omega Financial actionable insights into sales performance, helping identify growth opportunities and bottlenecks.

Results Achieved

1. **Significant Sales Growth:** The company saw a 45% increase in sales within the first year of implementation, driven by improved efficiency and focused sales efforts.
2. **Cost Savings:** By eliminating redundant processes and reducing errors, Omega Financial achieved substantial operational cost reductions.
3. **Stronger Customer Relationships:** Regular, personalized communication fostered by the CRM platform enhanced customer satisfaction and loyalty.
4. **Increased Team Productivity:** Automation and better resource allocation empowered the sales team to focus on strategic activities, leading to higher productivity.

Lessons Learned

Omega Financial's journey highlights the importance of aligning human expertise with technology to achieve transformational results. By addressing inefficiencies and empowering their team with the right tools, the company positioned itself as a more agile and competitive player in the wealth management space.

Key Takeaways for Sales Leaders

1. **Invest in the Right Technology:** A robust CRM can unify data, streamline operations, and provide actionable insights that drive growth.
2. **Foster Team Adoption:** Success with technology requires buy-in from your team. Training and demonstrating the benefits of new tools are crucial for adoption.
3. **Focus on the Customer:** Technology should enhance the customer experience, ensuring interactions are personalized and seamless.

Omega Financial's transformation underscores the critical role of sales leadership in navigating change, leveraging technology, and achieving lasting success in today's competitive landscape.

CHAPTER 2

Developing a Winning Sales Strategy

"Strategy without tactics is the slowest route to victory. Tactics without strategy are the noise before defeat."

– Sun Tzu

In the ever-evolving sales landscape, crafting a winning strategy isn't just important—it's foundational. A strong strategy provides the clarity and direction your team needs to navigate customer demands, industry shifts, and competitive pressures. As a senior sales leader, your role isn't only about setting the strategy but ensuring it permeates every level of the organization, driving measurable results.

This chapter offers a comprehensive approach to sales strategy development, emphasizing the interplay of data, technology, processes, people, and experience. By focusing on these pillars, you can empower your team to execute consistently, adapt rapidly, and exceed ambitious targets.

The Senior Sales Leader's Role in Strategy Development

A winning sales strategy begins with leadership. As a sales leader, your approach to strategy must balance vision with execution. While your team operates in the trenches, you are responsible for setting the direction, identifying barriers, and unlocking opportunities. Effective leaders adopt a "big picture" mindset, leveraging tools, data, and real-world insights to:

- **Drive alignment across the organization.** Ensure sales, marketing, and customer success teams operate under a unified strategy.
- **Equip your team with the right tools and training.** This includes not only technology but also fostering critical thinking and problem-solving skills.
- **Measure and refine.** Sales strategies must be agile, evolving as market dynamics shift.

Enhancing Sales Strategy with AI Tools

Turning Data into Actionable Insights

AI offers transformative potential by transforming raw data into actionable insights. For sales leaders, leveraging AI tools like Salesforce Einstein, Clari, and Tableau enables deeper visibility into performance metrics, customer behaviors, and market trends.

- **Improvement Focus:** Invest in training your team to interpret AI outputs effectively. It's not enough to have the tools; your team must understand how to apply insights to refine pitches, tailor campaigns, and prioritize leads.

Predicting and Preparing for Trends

AI-powered predictive analytics tools can help identify upcoming opportunities and threats. For example, using tools like SalesLoft to anticipate customer churn or new buying patterns can inform resource allocation and mitigate risks.

- **Improvement Focus:** Integrate predictive insights into team planning sessions. Create dashboards that dynamically update with key predictive metrics and teach managers to integrate them into weekly reviews.

Refining Strategic Planning with SWOT Analysis

A senior leader's perspective on SWOT analysis should go beyond listing strengths, weaknesses, opportunities, and threats. It's about connecting these elements to actionable plans.

Strengths

- **Leverage Your Unique Selling Proposition (USP):** Map your strengths to customer pain points. If your team excels in consultative selling, align strategies to complex sales opportunities where this strength adds value.
- **Improvement Focus:** Regularly revisit your perceived strengths to ensure they align with current market demands.

Weaknesses

- **Identify Bottlenecks and Gaps:** Conduct post-mortems on lost deals to uncover systemic weaknesses. Is your team equipped with the skills to counter competitor objections?
- **Improvement Focus:** Turn weaknesses into learning opportunities. For example, if long sales cycles are a challenge, implement time-to-value initiatives to drive quicker wins.

Opportunities

- **Capitalize on Market Trends:** Beyond identifying opportunities, prioritize them based on potential ROI. For instance, if sustainable solutions are trending, how can you adapt your messaging or products to meet this demand?
- **Improvement Focus:** Build rapid response teams to seize high-value opportunities quickly.

Threats

- **Proactive Mitigation:** Use AI tools to monitor competitive activity and market disruptions. Develop contingency plans for top threats.
- **Improvement Focus:** Make threat analysis an ongoing activity. Incorporate it into quarterly reviews, ensuring your strategy remains resilient.

Maximizing Technology for Sales Performance

As a senior sales leader, you must ensure that your team has access to tools that enhance performance while maintaining simplicity and integration.

Key Tools for Improvement

1. **Google Analytics:** For understanding customer behavior at the top of the funnel.
    - *Improvement Focus:* Use GA insights to refine lead-generation strategies and adjust the sales pipeline.
2. **HubSpot CRM:** To track pipeline activity and automate follow-ups.
    - *Improvement Focus:* Ensure data hygiene by conducting monthly audits of CRM entries.
3. **Monday.com:** For collaborative pipeline management and task automation.
    - *Improvement Focus:* Leverage automation features to reduce time spent on manual updates, allowing reps to focus on customer interactions.
4. **LinkedIn Sales Navigator:** To deepen prospecting efforts.
    - *Improvement Focus:* Train teams on advanced search techniques to unlock untapped lead pools.

Driving Execution Through Process Optimization

A strategy is only as good as its execution. Process optimization ensures that your team moves efficiently from lead generation to deal closure.

- **Define Key Milestones:** Break down the customer journey into actionable stages, ensuring clear handoffs between sales and customer success teams.
- **Automate Repetitive Tasks:** Use tools like Outreach.io to handle routine follow-ups, allowing reps to focus on relationship-building.
- **Improvement Focus:** Audit your sales processes quarterly. Gather feedback from reps and customers to identify friction points and refine workflows.

Fostering a Data-Driven Culture

As a senior sales leader, embedding a data-driven mindset across the team is critical. Equip your team to:

- **Use Metrics to Evaluate Performance:** Define KPIs that align with your strategy, such as customer acquisition costs, average deal size, and conversion rates.
- **Make Informed Adjustments:** Conduct bi-weekly data reviews to identify areas for improvement.
- **Improvement Focus:** Train team members on interpreting data through workshops or certifications in tools like Tableau or Power BI.

Leading by Example

The most successful sales leaders are those who exemplify the behaviors they wish to see. This includes:

- **Investing in Team Development:** Host regular skill-building sessions.

- **Championing Resilience:** In the face of adversity, show how to adapt and stay focused on long-term goals.
- **Improvement Focus:** Implement leadership shadowing, where junior leaders can observe and learn from your decision-making process.

Key Takeaways for Senior Sales Leaders

1. **Balance Strategy with Agility:** Regularly reassess your approach to align with changing market dynamics.
2. **Invest in Tools and Training:** Ensure your team has the resources and knowledge to succeed.
3. **Focus on Execution:** Drive clarity and consistency in your sales processes to maintain momentum.

By approaching sales strategy through the lens of a senior leader, you ensure not only the success of your team but also the lasting impact of your strategic vision.

CHAPTER 3

Building and Managing a High-Performing Sales Team

"Great things in business are never done by one person. They're done by a team of people."

– Steve Jobs.

In sales, no single individual can carry the weight of success alone. Behind every record-breaking quarter and every closed deal lies the strength of a well-coordinated, high-performing sales team. But building such a team is more than just finding talented individuals; it's about cultivating the right environment, setting clear expectations, and managing each person's strengths to achieve collective greatness.

This chapter is your guide to creating and leading a sales team that doesn't just meet expectations but consistently exceeds them. Whether you're starting from scratch or refining an existing team, the principles outlined here will help you build a powerhouse of sales professionals ready to take your organization to the next level.

Strategic Recruitment

The foundation of any high-performing sales team begins with strategic recruitment[1]. It's not just about finding individuals with impressive résumés; it's about assembling a team of professionals who possess the necessary skills, embody the company's core values, and seamlessly integrate into the existing culture. This strategic approach ensures long-term success, as employees who align with your company's mission and ethos are more likely to be motivated, productive, and loyal. Here's how to master the art of strategic recruitment[2]:

Develop Precise Job Descriptions

The first step in attracting top talent is to craft clear and precise job descriptions. A well-written job description does more than list the duties and qualifications; it paints a picture of the role, the company, and what success looks like within your team. You need to articulate the role's expectations, the key performance indicators (KPIs), and the skills required to excel. However, it's equally important to convey the broader context, including why this role matters to the company's goals and how it fits into the bigger picture.

For example, instead of simply listing "*sales experience required,*" explain the specific type of sales experience you're looking for. Is it B2B or B2C? Are you targeting enterprise clients or small businesses? What kinds of tools or CRM systems will they be expected to use? This clarity ensures that you attract candidates who not only meet the technical requirements but also understand and are prepared for the nuances of the role.

Additionally, your job description should reflect the company's values. Include phrases that highlight your organization's culture, such

---

[1] https://www.turing.com/resources/strategic-recruitment
[2] https://unstop.com/blog/behavioral-assessments-for-hiring

as *"team-oriented," "innovative,"* or *"customer-centric,"* to attract candidates who resonate with those qualities. The more precise and tailored your job description, the higher the likelihood of attracting candidates who fit both the role and your company culture.

Implement Behavioral Interviews

The interview process is crucial for uncovering a candidate's potential beyond their résumé. Behavioral interviews are a powerful tool for assessing how candidates might perform in real-life situations, particularly those that mirror the challenges they will face on your sales team. By asking situational questions, you can dig deeper into their thought processes, decision-making skills, and ability to align with your company's values.

For example, instead of asking, *"Tell me about a time you closed a big deal,"* you could ask, *"Describe a time when you faced a significant challenge in closing a deal. How did you approach it, and what was the outcome?"* This type of question assesses their problem-solving skills and reveals how they react under pressure and adapt to changing circumstances.

Behavioral interviews also give you insight into how candidates align with your company's core values. If teamwork is a core value, ask questions like, *"Can you provide an example of a time when you worked with a team to achieve a difficult sales target? What role did you play, and how did you support your team members?"* This approach allows you to see how well the candidate fits into the collaborative culture of your company.

By focusing on behavioral responses, you can better predict future performance and ensure that your new hires are skilled and aligned with the company's mission and values.

Skill Assessments

While interviews can give you a sense of a candidate's experiences and thought processes, skill assessments are essential for evaluating their practical abilities. This is especially important for sales roles, where the ability to execute is just as important as strategy or experience. Skill assessments give candidates the opportunity to demonstrate their real-world sales skills in a controlled environment.

For instance, you could incorporate role-playing exercises where candidates must simulate a sales pitch to a prospective client. This exercise allows you to assess their communication skills, persuasion techniques, and ability to think on their feet. It also gives insight into their style of selling, such as determining whether they are consultative, transactional, or relationship-focused. These insights can be crucial in determining whether their approach aligns with your sales team's philosophy.

In addition to role-playing, you might also consider assessments that test their ability to use the tools and technologies critical to your sales process. For example, if your company relies heavily on a CRM system, you could test their proficiency in navigating it, creating reports, or analyzing customer data. Practical tests like these ensure that your candidates not only talk the talk but can also walk the walk when it comes to the job's essential functions.

Cultural Fit Evaluation

Skills can be taught, but cultural alignment is often innate. Ensuring that a candidate fits well within your company's culture is just as important as their technical abilities. A strong cultural fit leads to better team dynamics, fosters long-term engagement, and reduces turnover. So, how do you assess cultural fit effectively?

First, it's crucial to have a deep understanding of your company's culture. What are the values that guide decision-making? How do employees collaborate and communicate? What is the company's stance on work-life balance, innovation, and personal development? Once you clearly understand these factors, you can incorporate them into the recruitment process.

One way to evaluate cultural fit is to include assessments or discussions exploring the candidate's values and work preferences. For instance, you can ask, "*What kind of work environment helps you thrive?*" or "*Tell me about a company culture you've previously enjoyed and why.*" These questions can help you gauge whether the candidate's expectations and values align with the environment you've cultivated within your sales team.

Additionally, consider having candidates meet with various members of the team during the interview process. This allows you to see how they interact with different personalities and gives your team a chance to provide feedback on whether the candidate would complement the existing dynamics.

You can also create hypothetical scenarios reflecting your company's values to see how candidates respond. For example, if one of your values is customer-centricity, you could ask, "*How would you handle a situation where a client has expressed dissatisfaction with our product or service?*" Their response will reveal how well they internalize and act upon the core values that drive your business.

Performance Management Software Integration

In today's data-driven sales environment, the integration of performance management software is crucial for effectively monitoring, analyzing, and enhancing sales team performance. The right software can streamline data management and provide real-time insights that allow leaders to make informed decisions, set clear objectives, and foster a culture of continuous improvement. By harnessing the power of performance management tools, sales leaders can ensure that their teams stay focused on goals while promoting accountability and motivation.

Select Appropriate Software

The first and perhaps most critical step in integrating performance management software is selecting the right tool for your team. The right software should seamlessly integrate with your existing systems, such as your CRM or communication platforms while offering customizable features to track the metrics that matter most to your business. This flexibility ensures that the software enhances your workflow rather than disrupting it or adding unnecessary complexity.

When choosing performance management software, consider factors such as ease of use, scalability, and the ability to generate detailed reports. Tools like **Workday**[3], **15Five**[4], or **BambooHR**[5] are popular choices that provide robust features for tracking individual and team performance. These platforms offer integrations with other sales tools, allowing you to gather data from various sources—such as sales figures, lead conversion rates, and customer feedback—into one unified system.

Customization is key. Every sales team is different, and your performance management software should allow you to tailor metrics and reports to fit your unique sales processes. For example, suppose your team focuses on long-term relationship-building. In that case, you might want software that tracks sales closures and metrics such as follow-up frequency and client satisfaction over time. The ability to customize ensures that the software aligns with your business priorities and provides actionable insights that drive meaningful improvements.

Set Transparent Objectives

Once the software is in place, it becomes a powerful tool for setting transparent and measurable objectives. With performance management software, you can define clear goals for each team member, aligned with the broader business outcomes you're striving to achieve. This transparency ensures that every sales rep knows exactly what is expected of them, reducing ambiguity and boosting accountability.

For instance, software like **Salesforce Performance Management**[6] or **Zoho People**[7] can help you set SMART goals (Specific, Measurable, Achievable, Relevant, and Time-bound) for each team

---

[3] https://www.workday.com/
[4] https://www.15five.com/
[5] https://www.bamboohr.com/
[6] https://www.salesforce.com/ap/sales/performance-management/
[7] https://www.zoho.com/people/

member. These goals could be tied to various sales metrics, such as monthly revenue targets, lead conversion rates, or client retention. Additionally, you can create tiered objectives that reflect different levels of experience within the team, ensuring that new hires and seasoned professionals are equally challenged and supported.

The advantage of using software for goal-setting is that it enables sales leaders to track progress in real-time. Dashboards provide visual representations of how individual team members perform against their targets, and managers can easily identify those exceeding expectations or falling behind. This real-time tracking allows for timely interventions, ensuring that underperformance is addressed early and that high achievers are recognized and rewarded.

Facilitate Ongoing Feedback

Gone are the days when annual or quarterly reviews were sufficient for managing sales performance. In a fast-paced sales environment, ongoing feedback is essential for continuous improvement, and performance management software can play a pivotal role in making this happen. Tools like **15Five** or **Lattice**[8] allow for continuous performance tracking and regular feedback loops, ensuring that sales reps receive the guidance and support they need throughout the year—not just during formal reviews.

With these tools, managers can establish regular check-ins and performance reviews based on software-generated data. For example, suppose a sales rep is consistently missing targets. In that case, the software will flag this trend, allowing the manager to provide immediate feedback and work with the rep to identify areas for improvement. Conversely, suppose a team member is consistently exceeding their

---

[8] https://lattice.com/

goals. In that case, this performance can be celebrated in real-time, boosting morale and setting a positive example for the rest of the team.

Additionally, performance management software enables peer-to-peer feedback, allowing team members to recognize each other's contributions. This fosters a collaborative environment where team members feel valued and supported, further enhancing team cohesion and overall performance. Giving and receiving real-time feedback also keeps communication lines open, allowing issues to be resolved quickly and preventing small problems from becoming major obstacles.

Implement Recognition Programs

One of the most powerful motivators in any sales team is recognition. Recognition of high performers for their efforts boosts morale and encourages continued excellence. Performance management software can be a game-changer in implementing recognition programs that are both data-driven and transparent, ensuring that recognition is based on merit and tied directly to performance metrics.

Software like **Reward Gateway**[9] or **Bonusly**[10] allows sales leaders to track individual achievements and provide tangible rewards to those who consistently exceed their goals, such as bonuses, gift cards, or public recognition. These platforms allow you to set up automated recognition programs that reward top performers in real-time based on criteria such as closing the highest number of deals, achieving the fastest conversion rate, or maintaining the best customer satisfaction scores.

By integrating recognition programs into your performance management software, you create a culture of healthy competition where everyone is motivated to push a little harder. However, it's essential to balance competition with collaboration. Performance management

---

[9] https://www.rewardgateway.com/
[10] https://bonusly.com/

tools can be used to promote team achievements as well, recognizing not only individual efforts but also the success of the team as a whole. This approach fosters a spirit of camaraderie and encourages sales reps to support each other in achieving collective goals.

Moreover, performance management software's transparency ensures that recognition is fair and objective. Everyone on the team can see how their performance compares to the established criteria, eliminating any perception of favoritism or bias. When sales reps know their hard work will be noticed and rewarded, they are likelier to remain engaged, motivated and committed to achieving their best.

Continuous Training and Development

In the ever-evolving world of sales, continuous training and development are crucial for maintaining a team that can keep up with market changes and thrive amidst technological advancements and shifting customer expectations. A high-performing sales team is one that is always learning, adapting, and improving. By investing in ongoing education, you're not just improving current performance—you're building a team that is resilient, innovative, and ready for future challenges. Here's how you can structure continuous training and development to keep your sales team ahead of the curve:

Conduct Regular Skills Audits

To build a truly adaptable sales force, you must first understand where your team stands in terms of skills and knowledge. Regular skills audits allow you to assess your sales team's training needs and identify both knowledge gaps and emerging skill requirements. This systematic evaluation helps sales leaders pinpoint where training is most needed, ensuring that development efforts are targeted and efficient.

For example, if your company has recently implemented a new CRM or sales automation tool, you'll need to ensure that all team members are proficient in using it. A skills audit could reveal who is struggling with and who has mastered the technology, allowing you to tailor your training sessions accordingly. Similarly, as market demands shift toward more digital sales or complex B2B relationships, you can identify the skills your team needs to develop to stay competitive, such as advanced negotiation techniques or digital marketing integration.

Skills audits can be done through assessments, one-on-one meetings, or even feedback from peers and managers. By conducting these audits regularly (quarterly or biannually), you can ensure that your team's skills remain sharp and relevant to the demands of your industry.

Adopt a Blended Learning Approach

Not everyone learns the same way, and in today's dynamic sales environment, a one-size-fits-all training method won't cut it. A blended learning approach combines multiple training formats to deliver a well-rounded and comprehensive learning experience. This methodology keeps the training engaging and flexible, catering to the diverse learning styles of your sales team.

Online Learning for Theory: E-learning platforms such as **Udemy, LinkedIn Learning,** or **Coursera** can provide self-paced modules on foundational sales theory, emerging market trends, and essential technologies. Online learning allows team members to absorb the theoretical knowledge they need at their own pace, making it a convenient option for busy sales professionals.

Workshops for Practical Application: While online learning is excellent for theory, practical application is key. Hands-on workshops, whether virtual or in-person, give your team the opportunity to practice new skills in a controlled environment. For instance, a workshop on objection-handling techniques could involve role-playing exercises where sales reps practice overcoming client objections with constructive feedback from their peers and instructors.

In-Person Seminars for Advanced Topics: Periodic in-person seminars or conferences can address more advanced or specialized topics requiring a deeper dive. These could include seminars on mastering the art of consultative selling, building strategic partnerships, or leveraging AI in sales. In-person learning is particularly effective for fostering team bonding and encouraging collaboration, as sales reps can share experiences and strategies in a more interactive setting.

By adopting a blended learning approach, you create a continuous learning environment that empowers your team to develop both theoretically and practically, ensuring they have the skills to succeed in every aspect of the sales process.

Update Training Materials Regularly

The world of sales is constantly evolving, and training materials that were effective a year ago might now be outdated. To keep your team competitive, ensuring that all training content reflects the latest industry trends, technologies, and sales techniques is critical. Updated materials keep your team aligned with current best practices and equip them to navigate new challenges confidently.

For example, suppose social selling has become more prevalent in your industry. In that case, your training materials should include updated content on how to build strong relationships through platforms like LinkedIn or Twitter. Similarly, if new regulations such as data privacy laws affect your sales process, your training programs must address these changes to ensure compliance.

Maintaining a feedback loop where team members and managers can suggest updates or new topics for inclusion is important. Use real-time data and customer feedback to adjust your training materials based on what's working in the field. Regularly reviewing your content, whether it's sales scripts, negotiation strategies, or technology tutorials, ensures your team is equipped with the most relevant tools to thrive.

Monitor and Evaluate Training Effectiveness

Training without measurement is like selling without a closing plan. To ensure your investment in training and development is paying off, you need to monitor and evaluate its effectiveness continuously.

Using assessments, performance data, and feedback loops, you can refine your training programs to ensure they are delivering the desired results.

Begin by setting clear, measurable goals for each training initiative. For example, if you're conducting a course on advanced sales techniques, you might set a target for a certain percentage increase in closed deals within a quarter. After the training, use tools like performance management software or sales dashboards to track progress toward these goals. Are the reps who completed the training closing more deals? Are they converting leads more efficiently?

Regular assessments, whether in the form of quizzes, peer evaluations, or role-playing exercises, can help you gauge whether the new skills are being applied effectively. Feedback from sales reps is also invaluable. It can be expanded if a certain training program consistently yields positive feedback and results. On the other hand, if performance doesn't improve after a training session, that may be a signal to revisit and refine the content or delivery method.

Data-Driven Decision Making

In today's competitive sales landscape, intuition alone isn't enough to stay ahead. Data-driven decision-making[11] has become a cornerstone of successful sales strategies, offering actionable insights that can optimize processes, enhance customer engagement, and forecast future trends. By leveraging data analytics, sales teams can move from reactive to proactive, making decisions based on concrete evidence rather than assumptions. Here's how you can master data-driven decision-making to supercharge your sales strategy.

---

[11] https://blog.hubspot.com/sales/data-in-sales

Comprehensive Data Collection

The foundation of any data-driven strategy is the quality of the data itself. To make informed decisions, you need to ensure comprehensive and accurate data capture at every stage of the sales process. This means collecting data from all customer touchpoints—from initial contact to post-sale follow-up—and ensuring that this data is organized, accessible, and regularly updated.

For example, a CRM system like HubSpot or Zoho CRM can track customer interactions across various channels, including emails, phone calls, social media, and website visits. By capturing this information in real-time, sales teams can gain a holistic view of each customer's journey, preferences, and pain points. It's crucial to standardize the data collection process so that every member of the team is inputting consistent information, whether it's a lead's job title, industry, or previous interactions with the company.

However, comprehensive data collection doesn't stop at customer interactions. It's also important to track internal sales activities—such as lead conversion rates, the average length of the sales cycle, and individual performance metrics for each sales rep. This complete picture allows sales leaders to understand what's working, what isn't, and where there are opportunities for improvement.

Utilize Advanced Analytical Tools

Data without analysis is just noise. To unlock the full potential of your sales data, you need to utilize advanced analytical tools that can process this information and reveal valuable insights. Tools like **Power BI, Tableau,** or **Google Data Studio** can visualize complex data sets, allowing sales leaders to identify patterns, trends, and performance metrics quickly.

These tools are designed to handle vast data and generate reports highlighting key metrics such as deal velocity, win/loss rates, and customer acquisition costs. For example, using **Power BI**, a sales leader can create dashboards that compare individual team members' performance against their targets, helping to identify top performers as well as those who may need additional support. Similarly, tools like **Tableau** can break down customer segmentation, revealing which demographics or industries are most responsive to your products or services.

Advanced analytical tools also allow for deeper dives into the data. Sales teams can use filtering options to segment data by region, product line, or even sales rep, making it easier to pinpoint areas of strength and opportunities for improvement. For instance, if a product line is performing poorly, analysis can reveal whether the issue is pricing, customer engagement, or market saturation. By leveraging these insights, sales leaders can make data-backed decisions to optimize sales tactics and resources.

Apply Insights to Strategy

Data becomes valuable when it is applied strategically. Once you've collected and analyzed your data, you can use those insights to fine-tune your sales strategy. Data-driven insights offer a clear picture of where your sales process is succeeding and where it's falling short, allowing you to make precise adjustments that yield better results.

For example, suppose the data shows that your sales team has a high win rate with prospects from a specific industry but struggles in others. In that case, you can allocate more resources toward that high-performing industry and tweak your approach for the lower-performing sectors. Similarly, suppose the data indicates that deals are consistently stalling at a particular stage in the pipeline. In that case, you can focus your training efforts on overcoming that hurdle—whether it's objection handling, follow-up cadence, or negotiation tactics.

Customer engagement strategies can also be personalized based on data insights. You can tailor your outreach to each prospect's specific needs by analyzing customer preferences and behavior patterns. If the data reveals that certain customers prefer a more consultative sales approach while others respond better to a direct sales pitch, your team can adjust their communication style accordingly. This level of personalization increases the likelihood of closing deals and strengthens long-term relationships with customers.

Moreover, applying data insights allows you to optimize pricing strategies, forecast revenue more accurately, and even improve team performance by identifying the sales reps' strengths and weaknesses. Turning data into actionable insights empowers your team to make smarter decisions that drive consistent growth.

Implement Predictive Analytics

While historical data provides valuable insights into past performance, predictive analytics offers a glimpse into the future. By employing predictive models, sales leaders can anticipate future market behaviors, customer needs, and trends, allowing them to stay ahead of the curve and adjust sales strategies proactively.

Predictive analytics tools like Clari or Salesforce Einstein use machine learning algorithms to analyze past sales data and identify patterns that can predict future outcomes. For instance, these tools can forecast which leads are most likely to convert based on their previous interactions, enabling sales teams to prioritize high-probability prospects and allocate resources more effectively. This allows sales leaders to focus on opportunities that are more likely to result in closed deals, improving overall conversion rates.

Moreover, predictive analytics can help forecast future revenue and set realistic sales targets. By analyzing seasonal trends, customer buying cycles, and market conditions, these tools provide sales leaders with the foresight needed to adjust their strategies. For example, suppose predictive models indicate a surge in demand for a particular product or service in the upcoming quarter. In that case, the sales team can prepare by ramping up outreach efforts, adjusting inventory levels, or tailoring marketing campaigns to capitalize on the anticipated growth.

Predictive analytics also plays a vital role in risk management. By identifying potential threats—such as a slowdown in a key market or increased competition—sales leaders can adjust their strategies in advance, mitigating the impact of external factors and keeping the team focused on sustainable growth.

Cultivating a High-Performance Culture

In any sales organization, culture is the invisible force that drives performance, shapes attitudes, and fuels long-term success. A high-performance culture[12] is one that not only sets high expectations but also creates an environment where individuals are empowered to meet and exceed them. This culture fosters collaboration, innovation, accountability, and continuous improvement—key ingredients for a sales team that consistently achieves its goals. Building such a culture requires deliberate action, clear communication, and a commitment to nurturing talent. Here's how you can cultivate a high-performance culture within your sales team.

Establish Clear Communication Channels

One of the foundational elements of a high-performance culture is communication. Without clear and open lines of communication, even the most talented sales team can become misaligned or disengaged. Promoting transparency across all levels of the organization ensures that every team member is informed, engaged, and aligned with the company's broader goals.

Open communication isn't just about sharing sales targets or reporting numbers; it's about creating a culture where feedback flows both ways. Sales leaders should provide regular updates on company strategy, sales objectives, and market changes, ensuring that every team member understands how their individual contributions fit into the bigger picture. This clarity gives sales reps a sense of purpose and ownership over their work, boosting motivation and engagement.

At the same time, it's important to establish mechanisms for team members to share their insights, ideas, and concerns. Whether it's through regular team meetings, one-on-one check-ins, or collaborative platforms like **Slack** or **Microsoft Teams**, creating opportunities for

---

[12] https://blog.hubspot.com/sales/sales-culture

open dialogue encourages team members to voice their thoughts and feel heard. This kind of transparency builds trust, fosters collaboration, and ensures that everyone is pulling in the same direction.

Encourage Innovation

A high-performance sales team thrives on innovation. To stay ahead in a competitive market, it's crucial to encourage team members to think outside the box, experiment with new approaches, and propose creative solutions. However, innovation requires an environment where individuals feel safe to take risks and experiment without fear of failure.

Creating a culture that embraces innovation starts with removing the stigma around mistakes. Sales leaders should promote the idea that failures are learning opportunities rather than setbacks. By framing failures as stepping stones to success, you encourage your team to test new strategies and refine their approach continuously. For example, a sales rep might experiment with a new social selling tactic or test a different sales script during cold calls. Even if these efforts don't immediately yield the desired results, the insights gained from experimentation are invaluable.

Sales teams can also benefit from collaborative brainstorming sessions where everyone is encouraged to share ideas, no matter how unconventional. By fostering a culture of curiosity and experimentation, you inspire your team to innovate, adapt, and find new ways to drive results.

Promote Leadership Development

Great leaders aren't just born—they're cultivated. To ensure the long-term success of your sales organization, it's important to identify and nurture potential leaders within your team. Leadership development should be a core component of your high-performance culture, as it prepares your team members to take on greater responsibility and inspire others to perform at their best.

Start by identifying individuals who demonstrate leadership potential—those who excel in their roles and exhibit strong communication skills, emotional intelligence, and a willingness to mentor others. Once identified, provide these individuals with opportunities for growth through mentorship programs, leadership training, and hands-on experience in leadership roles.

Mentorship programs, in particular, are an effective way to nurture leadership skills. Pairing high-potential team members with experienced sales leaders allows them to learn the nuances of leadership, from motivating a team to making strategic decisions. In addition, formal leadership training—whether through workshops, seminars, or online courses—can provide aspiring leaders with the tools they need to succeed in management roles.

By cultivating a pipeline of future leaders, you create a culture of continuous development where every team member has the opportunity to grow and contribute to the success of the organization.

Regularly Review and Adapt Sales Practices

A high-performance culture is one that embraces continuous improvement. The sales landscape is constantly evolving, and what worked yesterday may not be effective tomorrow. To stay ahead, it's essential to regularly review and adapt your sales practices, ensuring they remain aligned with industry best practices and the ever-changing needs of your customers.

Start by conducting regular assessments of your team's performance, identifying areas where they excel and areas that need improvement. Use data analytics to track key metrics—such as win/loss rates, sales cycle length, and lead conversion rates—and compare these metrics against industry benchmarks. This data-driven approach allows you to identify patterns, spot potential issues, and make informed decisions about where adjustments are needed.

In addition to performance assessments, it's important to keep a pulse on broader industry trends. New technologies, customer expectations, and market dynamics are constantly emerging, and your sales team needs to adapt accordingly. Whether it's adopting new sales enablement tools, refining your messaging to align with shifting customer priorities or incorporating more personalized selling techniques, regular adaptation ensures that your team remains competitive and effective.

Furthermore, involve your team in the review process. Ask for their feedback on current sales practices, encourage them to share what's working and what's not, and collaborate on ways to improve. This inclusive approach fosters a sense of ownership and empowers team members to contribute to the organization's continuous improvement.

In conclusion, by systematically applying the processes and methodologies outlined in this chapter, sales leaders can foster the development of a high-performing team that consistently meets—and even exceeds—sales targets. From strategic recruitment to integrating performance management software, continuous training, and leveraging data-driven insights, each step is designed to build a team that is successful in the short term and resilient in the face of change. A well-rounded approach that fosters innovation, promotes leadership development and cultivates a high-performance culture ensures that your team remains adaptable, motivated, and ready to tackle any challenge.

Ultimately, the goal is to create a sales team that thrives in today's fast-paced, competitive business environment. As market conditions shift and customer expectations evolve, sales teams that are equipped with the right tools, skills, and mindset will be the ones to seize opportunities and drive sustained growth. By leading with intent and adopting these best practices, you position your team—and your organization—for long-term success in an ever-changing landscape.

CHAPTER 4

Implementing Effective Sales Techniques

"Success is where preparation and opportunity meet."

– **Bobby Unser.**

In the dynamic world of sales, preparation means more than just understanding your product; it's about mastering the right techniques to create meaningful connections and drive results. Implementing effective sales techniques is not just a matter of skill but of strategy, ensuring that each interaction leaves a lasting impression and builds a foundation for long-term success.

This chapter will explore the most impactful sales techniques and how they can be adapted for different contexts and industries. Whether you're selling a service, product, or idea, knowing when and how to apply these techniques is key to staying ahead in today's competitive marketplace.

Consultative Selling

Consultative selling[13] is a powerful approach that focuses on building long-term relationships and delivering tailored solutions rather than just closing a deal. It's about shifting from a transactional mindset to one of partnership, where the sales professional becomes a trusted advisor. This technique is deeply rooted in understanding the customer's unique challenges, aspirations, and overall goals and then guiding them toward the best possible solution. Unlike traditional sales approaches that focus on pushing products, consultative selling centers on the customer's needs, providing them with real value.

1. Understanding Customer Needs

The foundation of consultative selling lies in deeply understanding the customer's needs, challenges, and desires. This begins by asking open-ended questions, encouraging the customer to share detailed information about their pain points and what they hope to achieve. Questions like, "What challenges are you currently facing?" or "What would success look like for you?" allow you to uncover the deeper issues driving the customer's buying decision. This phase requires active listening and empathy, as the more you understand, the better equipped you'll be to offer valuable insights and solutions.

Active listening goes beyond simply hearing the customer's words—it involves picking up on underlying concerns and emotions, reading between the lines, and showing that you genuinely care about their success. By demonstrating a deep understanding of their business or personal challenges, you begin to earn their trust, positioning yourself as someone who can help them solve real problems.

---

[13] https://www.pipedrive.com/en/blog/consultative-selling

2. Building Relationships

Trust is the cornerstone of consultative selling, and building strong relationships is key to earning that trust. Customers are far more likely to do business with someone they feel genuinely cares about their success. This is why consultative selling places such a heavy emphasis on rapport-building. Instead of immediately jumping into product details or price negotiations, take the time to get to know your customer deeper—what drives them, their goals, and how they like to do business.

Building relationships also means demonstrating reliability. Follow through on your promises, provide regular updates, and be proactive in addressing any concerns. When customers feel that you have their best interests at heart, they'll view you as more than just a salesperson—they'll see you as a trusted advisor and partner.

3. Tailored Solutions

The hallmark of consultative selling is the ability to offer tailored solutions that directly address the customer's unique needs. After gaining a thorough understanding of their challenges, you can then present a product or service that is customized to their specific situation. This personalized approach shows the customer that you're not just trying to make a sale but are invested in helping them succeed.

For instance, if you're selling B2B technology solutions, rather than pitching a one-size-fits-all product, you might propose a customized software package that addresses the exact pain points the customer mentioned—whether it's improving operational efficiency, enhancing customer experience, or reducing costs. The more personalized and relevant the solution, the more value the customer will perceive, making them more likely to choose your offering over a competitor's generic solution.

Best Fit: Consultative selling is particularly effective in industries where the buying process is complex, such as B2B technology, professional services, and high-value financial products. These sectors often require highly customized solutions that meet specific client needs, making consultative selling a perfect fit.

Solution Selling

Solution selling shares several similarities with consultative selling but with a key difference: it focuses on providing a predefined solution to a problem the customer has already identified. While consultative selling emphasizes diagnosing the customer's needs, solution selling[14] assumes the customer is already aware of their problem and is looking for a targeted solution. This technique is efficient and direct, guiding the customer toward a specific product or service that addresses their known issue.

1. Identifying the Problem

Before presenting any solution, it's crucial to ensure that both you and the customer are on the same page regarding their problem. Start by asking clarifying questions to ensure the issue is well understood by the customer and you as the sales professional. This step helps confirm the problem and sets the stage for presenting your solution.

For example, if you're selling a healthcare solution to a medical practice, the customer might have already identified a need for more efficient patient management. By confirming this need and understanding its scope—perhaps they are overwhelmed by administrative tasks—you can then move forward with presenting a product that solves this specific challenge.

2. Presenting the Solution

Once the problem is clearly defined, it's time to present the solution. The key here is to be direct and focused—show the customer how your product or service directly addresses their issue. Instead of

[14] https://www.helpscout.com/blog/solution-selling/

offering a broad overview of your solution's features, focus on the ones most relevant to the customer's problem. The more concise and tailored your presentation, the more likely the customer is to see the immediate value in your solution.

For instance, if you're offering a software solution for the healthcare practice, demonstrate how your product's patient management system can save them time, reduce errors, and streamline their operations. Show them exactly how your solution alleviates the pain points they've already recognized.

3. Demonstrating Value

The final and most critical step in solution selling is clearly demonstrating the value of your offering. It's not enough to say that your product solves the problem—you need to show the customer the concrete benefits and the return on investment they can expect. Use case studies, testimonials, and data to back up your claims, making it clear that your solution not only resolves their issue but also delivers measurable value.

For example, you might share a success story about a similar healthcare practice that implemented your software and saw a 30% increase in operational efficiency. Demonstrating that your solution has a proven track record of success reinforces its value and builds the customer's confidence in their decision.

Best Fit: Solution selling works best in industries where customers have a clear, identifiable problem that needs solving. This approach is common in software sales, healthcare solutions, and engineering services, where buyers often have a specific issue they need to address and are looking for an effective, straightforward solution.

Upselling

Upselling is a sales technique focused on encouraging customers to purchase a higher-end version of a product or service than they originally intended. This approach works by capitalizing on the customer's initial interest, showing them how additional features, upgrades, or premium options can enhance their experience. The key to successful upselling[15] is offering added value that aligns with the customer's needs and delivering that pitch at the right moment.

1. Understanding Customer Needs

Effective upselling starts with a solid understanding of what the customer values. Before suggesting any upgrades, you need to know what's most important to them—whether it's quality, convenience, performance, or status. By identifying these preferences, you can tailor your upsell to highlight the features or benefits that matter most to the customer.

For example, suppose a customer is purchasing a smartphone and values top-notch camera quality. In that case, you can introduce them to the higher-end model with superior camera features, positioning it as the perfect upgrade to meet their specific need.

2. Presenting Upgrades

Once you understand the customer's priorities, it's time to present the upgrade. When upselling, the focus should be on how the upgraded version will enhance the customer's overall experience. Emphasize the added value—whether it's improved functionality, extended service, or premium features—and explain how these benefits align with what the customer is already looking for.

For instance, when upselling in the subscription services industry, you could highlight the added convenience of premium support or exclusive content available only to higher-tier subscribers. The goal is to make the customer see the upgrade as a natural extension of their initial purchase, not an unnecessary add-on.

---

[15] https://www.salesforce.com/eu/learning-centre/sales/upselling/

3. Timing

Timing is critical when upselling. The best opportunities arise when the customer is already engaged and close to making a purchase decision. At this point, they've already recognized your product's or service's value, and introducing an upgrade feels like a logical next step rather than a hard sell. Offering the upsell too early in the process can feel pushy while introducing it too late might miss the moment when the customer is most open to considering additional options.

For example, when a customer is finalizing their order or about to check out, it's the perfect time to offer a higher-end version of the product or an extended service plan that complements their purchase. The customer is already mentally committed, making them more receptive to suggestions that enhance their original choice.

Best Fit: Upselling is particularly effective in industries such as consumer goods, electronics, and subscription services, where customers frequently seek premium features or higher levels of service. In these sectors, customers are often willing to invest more if they perceive the added value as beneficial to their experience.

Cross-Selling

Cross-selling is an effective technique that helps sales professionals increase the value of a sale by suggesting complementary products or services. The key to successful cross-selling[16] is ensuring that the additional items enhance the primary purchase and provide real value to the customer. When executed correctly, cross-selling doesn't feel like an upsell; instead, it feels like a thoughtful recommendation that enriches the customer's experience.

---

[16] https://www.zendesk.com/blog/upselling-and-cross-selling-strategy/

1. Understanding the Primary Purchase

The foundation of cross-selling is rooted in a deep understanding of the customer's initial purchase. Before suggesting complementary products, you must identify the main product or service the customer is buying and fully understand how they intend to use it. By doing this, you can more accurately determine which additional items will enhance the value of their purchase.

For example, if a customer is purchasing a laptop, understanding whether they'll be using it for business, gaming, or design work will help guide your cross-selling recommendations. Someone using the laptop for creative work may benefit from software that enhances design capabilities, while a business user may need a docking station or extra storage. Knowing how the primary purchase fits into the customer's life allows you to make relevant and valuable suggestions.

2. Suggesting Complementary Products

Once you understand the customer's primary purchase, the next step is to suggest complementary products or services that enhance their overall experience. These could include accessories, service plans, or add-ons that are directly related to the main item. The key to successful cross-selling is to position these suggestions as beneficial, not as an upsell, to increase sales.

For instance, if a customer is purchasing a smartphone, suggesting a protective case, wireless earbuds, or an extended warranty can add value to their purchase. These products complement the phone and improve the customer's experience, ensuring that their investment is protected and more enjoyable.

3. Providing Value

Above all, cross-selling must be about providing genuine value to the customer. The additional products or services you suggest should seamlessly fit into their original purchase, solving potential problems or enhancing convenience. If the customer perceives the cross-sell as something that will improve their experience or help them get more out of their purchase, they are far more likely to take advantage of the offer.

For example, a customer buying a camera may not realize the benefits of having a high-quality memory card or additional lenses. By explaining how these accessories can improve their camera performance and offer greater flexibility, you demonstrate the value of cross-selling. It's not about pushing for a larger sale but about enhancing the customer's satisfaction with their purchase.

Best Fit: Cross-selling is highly effective in industries such as retail, e-commerce, and services where complementary products or add-ons can significantly enhance the customer's experience. Think of products like electronics, beauty supplies, and travel services, where customers often benefit from additional purchases that support their main investment.

Inbound Selling

Inbound selling is a modern approach that capitalizes on warm leads generated through marketing efforts such as content creation, SEO, and social media. Instead of chasing cold prospects, inbound selling involves converting customers who have already shown an interest in your product or service by engaging with your content. The key to success in inbound selling[17] is nurturing these leads through the funnel, providing them with valuable information and personalized solutions along the way.

1. Attracting Leads

Inbound selling begins with attracting potential customers to your brand through content marketing, social media, and SEO. The idea is to create valuable and relevant content that speaks to your audience's needs and positions your company as an authority in the field.

---

[17] https://www.yesware.com/blog/inbound-selling/

Whether it's blog posts, white papers, or videos, this content acts as a magnet, drawing in prospects already interested in your offer.

For example, a digital marketing agency might publish articles or videos on how to optimize online ad campaigns, attracting businesses looking for that exact service. You establish trust and credibility by providing valuable content, making potential customers more likely to engage with your company.

2. Engaging with Leads

Once potential customers have engaged with your content, it's time to interact with them directly. This engagement often starts with offering more personalized content, such as webinars, demos, or downloadable resources that address specific challenges. It's important to continue providing value while guiding the lead through the sales process.

For instance, if someone downloads a guide on increasing conversion rates, follow up with an email offering a free consultation on how your product or service can help them apply the strategies outlined in the guide. The goal is to build a relationship by addressing their needs and offering tailored solutions rather than pushing for an immediate sale.

3. Converting Leads

The final step in inbound selling is converting those engaged leads into customers. By this point, the prospect is likely well-informed about your product or service and understands how it can solve their specific problem. Your role is to guide them through the decision-making process, offering additional support and personalized recommendations to seal the deal.

For example, a SaaS provider might offer a free trial to a lead who has engaged with multiple pieces of content, allowing them to experience the platform firsthand. Inbound selling helps you turn warm leads into loyal customers by offering relevant solutions and addressing any lingering concerns.

Best Fit: Inbound selling is highly effective in industries with a strong online presence and content-driven marketing strategies, such as digital marketing agencies, SaaS providers, and e-commerce businesses.

Outbound Selling

Outbound selling is the more traditional sales approach, involving proactively reaching out to potential customers who may not yet be aware of your product or service. It's a technique used to generate new leads and create opportunities where they may not have existed before. Outbound selling[18] requires targeted efforts, personalized messaging, and persistence to convert prospects into customers.

1. Targeting Prospects

The success of outbound selling hinges on identifying the right prospects. Before initiating any outreach, it's essential to research potential customers who would benefit most from your product or service. This means analyzing market segments, identifying pain points, and focusing on those most likely to respond positively to your outreach efforts.

For example, a B2B software company targeting mid-sized manufacturing firms may research prospects by industry, company size, and revenue. By narrowing down the ideal customer profile, you can craft a more effective outreach strategy that resonates with your target audience.

2. Crafting Outreach Messages

Once you've identified your prospects, the next step is to craft personalized and compelling messages that capture their attention. Whether you're reaching out via email, phone, or direct mail, your

[18] https://www.cognism.com/outbound-sales-software

message should address your prospect's specific challenges and highlight how your product or service can solve them.

For instance, if you're reaching out to real estate developers, your message might focus on how your construction management software streamlines workflows and reduces costs. Personalization is key here—demonstrating that you understand their unique needs makes your outreach more impactful and increases the chances of a positive response.

3. Follow-Up

Outbound selling doesn't end after the first contact. Following up consistently is crucial to nurturing relationships and moving prospects through the sales funnel. Many sales are won not on the first attempt but after several touchpoints, so persistence and timing are essential.

For example, after sending an introductory email, you might follow up with a phone call a few days later to check in and offer additional information. Regular follow-up and value-driven messaging keep the conversation going and show prospects that you're committed to helping them find the right solution.

Best Fit: Outbound selling is particularly effective in industries where proactive lead generation is essential, such as B2B sales, real estate, and high-ticket item sales. It's ideal for sales environments where the customer may not be aware of your offering but could see significant value once educated.

SPIN Selling

SPIN Selling is a consultative sales technique that uses a series of questions to uncover the customer's needs and demonstrate how your product or service can address their specific challenges. Developed by Neil Rackham, SPIN stands for Situation, Problem, Implication, and

Need-Payoff, with each type of question guiding the conversation toward a solution. SPIN Selling[19] is particularly effective in complex sales environments where deep understanding and tailored solutions are critical.

1. Situation Questions

SPIN Selling begins with Situation questions designed to gather information about the customer's current circumstances. These questions help set the stage for deeper conversations by giving you a better understanding of the customer's context.

For example, a Situation question might be: "How are you currently managing your inventory?" or "What software are you using for project management?" These questions establish a baseline understanding of where the customer is now, allowing you to identify potential areas for improvement.

2. Problem Questions

Next, Problem questions are used to uncover the customer's specific challenges or pain points. By identifying these problems, you can start to position your product or service as the solution.

For instance, you might ask, "What issues are you encountering with your current inventory management system?" or "Have you faced any challenges with project deadlines due to inefficiencies?" Problem questions allow the customer to express their frustrations, which creates an opportunity for you to offer a solution.

3. Implication Questions

Implication questions dig deeper by exploring the consequences of the customer's problems. These questions are designed to highlight the impact of the challenges on the customer's business or life, making

---

[19] https://blog.hubspot.com/sales/spin-selling-the-ultimate-guide

the problems more pressing and motivating the customer to seek a solution.

For example, you might ask, "How does the inefficiency in your inventory system affect your ability to meet customer demand?" or "What are the financial implications of missing project deadlines?" By focusing on the implications, you encourage the customer to recognize the urgency of resolving their issues.

4. Need-Payoff Questions

Finally, Need-Payoff questions focus on the benefits of solving the problem. These questions help the customer envision how your product or service can provide value and improve their situation.

For instance, you could ask, "How would streamlining your inventory management improve your operations and customer satisfaction?" or "How would meeting project deadlines more consistently impact your bottom line?" These questions lead the customer to see the value in your offering and make it easier for them to justify the purchase.

Best Fit: SPIN Selling is best suited for complex sales environments, such as enterprise sales and consulting services, where understanding the customer's unique challenges is critical to positioning your product as the right solution. This technique works well when a deep understanding of the customer's needs and a tailored approach are necessary for closing the deal.

Challenger Selling

Challenger Selling is a dynamic technique that shifts the traditional sales approach from simply addressing customer needs to challenging their perspectives and teaching them something new about their business. Rather than waiting for customers to recognize a problem, Challenger Selling[20] takes a proactive stance, providing unique insights and sparking a shift in the customer's thinking. This method is particularly effective when dealing with complex products or services that require a deep understanding of the market.

1. Teaching

The core of Challenger Selling is teaching the customer something they didn't know about their business or market. This involves offering insights that change how they think about their current situation or the challenges they face. Successful Challenger Sellers don't just present data—they provide a fresh perspective that reframes the customer's understanding of their industry and positions your solution as essential for future success.

For instance, if you're selling cybersecurity solutions, instead of just explaining the features of your software, you might educate the customer on emerging threats in their industry and how their current systems are vulnerable. By doing so, you provide value beyond the product itself—you're helping the customer see risks they hadn't considered and positioning your offering as the solution to a problem they didn't fully understand.

2. Tailoring

Challenger Selling is not a one-size-fits-all approach; it requires customization based on the customer's specific needs, goals, and circumstances. After introducing new insights, you need to tailor your message to align with the customer's unique situation. This involves understanding their business model, industry challenges, and strategic objectives and then adapting your solution to fit these needs.

---

[20] https://www.pipedrive.com/en/blog/challenger-sales-model

For example, suppose you're speaking with a financial services firm. In that case, you might focus on how the economic landscape is shifting and how your solution helps them stay agile in times of market volatility. By tailoring your message to their specific context, you ensure that the insights you provide are relevant and actionable, making it easier for the customer to see the value in your solution.

3. Taking Control

Challenger Selling also requires sales professionals to take control of the conversation. This doesn't mean being pushy; it means confidently guiding the customer through the buying process and addressing objections with authority. By taking control, you help the customer move through their decision-making process more efficiently, ensuring that their concerns are addressed and that they see the value in taking action.

When a customer hesitates, a Challenger Seller doesn't retreat but provides additional insights to overcome objections. For example, if the customer is worried about the cost of your solution, you could point out the long-term savings or competitive advantages it provides, reframing the conversation around value rather than price.

Best Fit: Challenger Selling is most effective in industries where products or services are complex and require a high level of education, such as high-tech industries, financial services, and consulting. This approach is ideal when customers need to be challenged in their thinking to recognize the value of a new solution.

Social Selling

Social selling leverages the power of social media platforms to connect with potential customers, build relationships, and ultimately drive sales. Unlike traditional selling, which often involves cold outreach, social selling[21] focuses on engaging with prospects in a more organic, relationship-driven way. It's about being present where your customers are (on social platforms) and providing value through thought leadership, insights, and genuine interaction.

1. Building Relationships

Social selling is, first and foremost, about relationship building. Rather than diving straight into a sales pitch, social sellers engage with potential customers by sharing relevant content, participating in conversations, and offering helpful advice. Platforms like LinkedIn, Twitter, and even Instagram allow sales professionals to connect with prospects in a non-intrusive way, nurturing relationships over time.

For example, suppose you're in the technology sector. In that case, you might share articles on industry trends, comment on posts related to emerging technologies, or offer advice in LinkedIn groups where your target audience congregates. By consistently providing value, you build credibility and trust, which positions you as a go-to resource when prospects are ready to make a buying decision.

2. Establishing Credibility

One of the key goals of social selling is establishing yourself as a credible authority in your field. To do this, sharing insights and thought leadership that demonstrate your expertise is important. This might include posting original content, such as blog articles or videos, or sharing relevant industry news and providing your perspective on it. The more value you provide, the more prospects will see you as an expert, which makes them more likely to engage with you when they're in the market for your product or service.

---

[21] https://sproutsocial.com/glossary/social-selling/

For instance, if you're a professional in the financial services industry, regularly sharing insights on market trends, investment strategies, or regulatory changes will position you as a knowledgeable expert. As your audience grows, you'll naturally attract prospects who are interested in your expertise and the solutions you offer.

3. Driving Sales

The ultimate goal of social selling is to convert relationships into sales. Once you've built trust and established credibility, you can begin to nurture leads by answering questions, addressing concerns, and providing more information about your product or service. Social selling is often a longer-term strategy compared to traditional outbound methods, but the relationships you build are more meaningful, and the leads are often warmer and more receptive to your offering.

For example, after engaging with a prospect on LinkedIn and providing insights over time, you can transition to a private message to offer a demo or consultation. Because the prospect already knows and trusts you, they're more likely to respond positively and move forward in the buying process.

Best Fit: Social selling works best in industries where establishing an online presence and credibility is key, such as technology, professional services, and consumer goods. It's particularly effective for companies with a strong online presence and a focus on content marketing.

Behavioral Selling

Behavioral selling[22] tailors the sales approach based on a deep understanding of the customer's behavior. This technique involves analyzing data related to purchasing habits, engagement with content, and interactions with your brand, allowing you to personalize your sales

---

[22] https://blog.discinsights.com/how-behavioral-selling-can-help-your-business

strategy and offer solutions that align with the customer's preferences and needs. Behavioral selling is all about using data to anticipate customer desires and provide a more customized experience.

1. Analyzing Behavior

The first step in behavioral selling is gathering and analyzing data on customer behavior. This might include tracking how customers interact with your website, engage with email campaigns, or respond to social media posts. By analyzing this data, you can gain valuable insights into what drives customer interest and how they make purchasing decisions.

For example, if you're in e-commerce, you might notice that a certain segment of your customer base tends to purchase after viewing multiple product pages, but only if they receive a discount offer. With this insight, you can tailor your approach by offering targeted discounts to these customers at the right moment, increasing the likelihood of conversion.

2. Personalizing Approach

Once you clearly understand the customer's behavior, you can personalize your sales approach to match their preferences. This might involve tailoring your messaging, adjusting your timing, or offering specific products that align with their interests. The more personalized your approach, the more likely you are to resonate with the customer and move them toward a purchase decision.

For instance, if a subscription service customer frequently engages with content about premium features but hasn't upgraded yet, you might send them a personalized email highlighting how the premium features address their specific needs. Personalization increases engagement and fosters a stronger connection between the customer and your brand.

3. Adapting Strategies

Customer behavior is constantly evolving, and successful behavioral selling requires continuous adaptation. By regularly reviewing customer data, you can adjust your strategies to align with their changing preferences and behaviors. This adaptability ensures that your sales approach remains relevant and effective, even as customer expectations shift.

For example, suppose you notice that a segment of customers is now engaging more with mobile content than desktop. In that case, you might adapt your marketing strategy to focus on mobile-first design and mobile-specific offers. Staying flexible and responsive to behavioral shifts ensures that you remain connected with your customers in the ways that matter most to them.

Best Fit: Behavioral selling is particularly effective in industries like e-commerce, subscription services, and digital marketing, where understanding customer behavior is crucial to delivering personalized experiences that drive sales.

Value-Based Selling

Value-based selling is a technique that focuses on the value your product or service provides rather than its features or price. Instead of simply discussing what your product does, value-based selling emphasizes how your offering delivers measurable benefits that align with the customer's goals. This approach helps customers see the long-term impact of your solution on their success, making it easier for them to justify the investment.

1. Highlighting Value

The cornerstone of value-based selling[23] is clearly articulating how your product or service delivers real, tangible value to the customer. This means going beyond listing features and instead focusing on the outcomes those features provide. For example, rather than saying,

[23] https://www.sales-i.com/blog/value-selling-and-why-its-important

"Our software automates data entry," you would say, "Our software reduces data entry time by 50%, allowing your team to focus on higher-value tasks."

By framing your offering in terms of value, you help the customer see how your product or service directly contributes to their success, whether it's by improving efficiency, increasing revenue, or reducing costs.

2. Quantifying Impact

One of the most powerful aspects of value-based selling is the ability to quantify the impact of your offering. This might involve providing data, case studies, or ROI calculations demonstrating your product's or service's real-world benefits. The more specific and measurable the value you provide, the easier it is for the customer to see how your solution can help them achieve their goals.

For instance, if you're selling enterprise software, you might provide a case study showing how a previous client reduced operating costs by 20% after implementing your solution. By presenting hard data, you strengthen your value proposition and give the customer confidence in their decision to invest in your product.

3. Focusing on Outcomes

Ultimately, value-based selling is about focusing on the outcomes your customer will achieve by using your product or service. This means shifting the conversation from the "what" (features) to the "why" (benefits). By emphasizing the positive outcomes your customer can expect—whether it's increased efficiency, enhanced performance, or improved profitability—you make it easier for them to envision how your offering fits into their long-term success.

For example, in the consulting industry, rather than discussing the steps you'll take during a project, you would focus on the results, such as how your recommendations will increase profitability or improve market share. By framing the conversation around outcomes, you reinforce the value you bring to the table.

Best Fit: Value-based selling is ideal for industries where customers are focused on outcomes and ROI, such as enterprise software, consulting services, and high-value investments. This technique is particularly effective when customers need to see a clear connection between their investment and the tangible results they'll achieve.

Referral Selling

Referral selling leverages the power of satisfied customers to generate new leads and drive sales through word-of-mouth recommendations. This technique is built on trust between you and your existing customers and between those customers and the new prospects they refer. By turning happy clients into advocates, referral selling[24] allows you to tap into an established network of credibility, making it easier to build relationships and close deals. It's particularly effective in industries where personal trust and relationship-building are key.

1. Building Referral Programs

A successful referral selling strategy begins with a formal, structured referral program. This program incentivizes both referrers and new customers, creating a win-win scenario where everyone benefits. When designing a referral program, think about what would motivate your existing customers to recommend your business. It could be discounts, cash rewards, exclusive offers, or even loyalty points that accumulate over time. At the same time, it offers something of value to new customers as an added incentive to encourage them to take action.

For example, a referral program in real estate might offer a monetary bonus to clients who refer new buyers or sellers. Similarly, a consultancy might provide discounted services to both the referrer and the new client in professional services. By structuring the program to make

---

[24] https://www.5percentinstitute.com/referral-selling-harness-word-of-mouth/

both parties feel valued, you increase the likelihood of referrals flowing in consistently.

2. Requesting Referrals

Even with a well-structured program, referrals won't come unless you ask for them. Actively requesting referrals from satisfied customers is a critical part of the process. The best time to ask for referrals is shortly after a positive interaction, such as when a customer expresses satisfaction with your service or when you've recently completed a successful project.

To make it easy for your customers to refer you, provide them with the tools they need—whether it's a simple referral form, a template email they can send to friends and colleagues, or a digital referral link they can share on social media. The easier you make it for customers to refer you, the more likely they'll be to do so.

3. Tracking and Rewarding

Once your referral program is in place, tracking its performance and ensuring that referrers are rewarded promptly is essential. By keeping a close eye on who is participating and how their referrals are converting into new business, you can make adjustments to optimize the program. Rewarding referrers consistently and visibly will encourage them to continue referring others, creating a positive feedback loop.

For example, if you run a luxury goods business, you could send a personalized thank-you note and reward to a client who referred a friend who made a purchase. This recognition fosters loyalty and incentivizes them to refer more clients in the future.

Best Fit: Referral selling is highly effective in industries where trust and word-of-mouth recommendations are crucial, such as professional services, real estate, and high-end consumer goods. In these fields, a personal endorsement from a trusted source can significantly influence the buying decision.

Storytelling

Storytelling is a powerful sales technique that taps into the emotional side of decision-making. Rather than simply listing features and benefits, storytelling[25] involves creating compelling narratives that resonate with the customer and show how your product or service can solve their problems or enhance their lives. This approach fosters deeper connections with potential customers, making your brand and offering more memorable.

1. Crafting Compelling Stories

At the heart of storytelling is the ability to craft a narrative that resonates with your target audience. The story should be centered around the customer's challenges, desires, and goals, showing how your product or service fits into their journey. Whether it's a case study of a past client's success or an imaginative scenario that highlights the benefits of your offering, the story should be relatable and engaging.

For example, a skincare brand might tell the story of a customer who struggled with sensitive skin for years before finding relief with their products. By focusing on the emotional and personal aspects of the customer's experience, the brand creates a story that potential buyers can see themselves in, making the product feel more relevant to their own lives.

2. Engaging Emotions

One of the most effective aspects of storytelling is its ability to evoke emotions. Emotions are a driving force behind purchasing decisions, and storytelling allows you to connect with customers on a deeper level by appealing to their desires, fears, or aspirations. Stories tap into what matters most to the customer, whether it's the joy of

---

[25] https://www.breakcold.com/explain/storytelling-in-sales

overcoming a challenge, the relief of solving a long-standing problem, or the excitement of achieving a goal.

For instance, movie trailers often use storytelling in the entertainment industry to evoke emotions, pulling viewers into a narrative that makes them feel excitement, tension, or curiosity. This emotional connection makes the audience more invested in the story and the product being sold.

3. Demonstrating Value

While storytelling is a great way to engage emotions, it's also a way to demonstrate your product or service's value clearly. Through the narrative, you show how your offering solves problems or improves the customer's life. The story should always circle back to the benefits of your product, ensuring that the audience understands not just the emotional appeal but also the practical value.

For example, a tech company selling project management software could tell the story of a team that was struggling with deadlines and communication until they implemented the software. The narrative would highlight the transformation, showing how the software improved collaboration, streamlined tasks, and ultimately led to successful project completion.

Best Fit: Storytelling is particularly effective in industries where emotional connection and brand narrative are essential, such as consumer goods, entertainment, and lifestyle products. It's also useful when selling products or services that are deeply personal or experiential.

Direct Selling

Direct selling[26] involves selling products directly to consumers outside of traditional retail environments. Whether through face-to-face interactions, events, or virtual platforms, this technique emphasizes personal relationships and tailored experiences. It's about connecting directly with the customer, understanding their needs, and offering customized solutions.

1. Personal Interaction

One of the key strengths of direct selling is the ability to engage with customers on a personal level. Whether it's a face-to-face meeting, a home demonstration, or a virtual event, direct selling allows salespeople to build relationships and provide personalized attention. This personal interaction builds trust and enables a more customized sales experience.

For example, a direct sales consultant selling beauty products might host a small in-person gathering where attendees can try the products firsthand, ask questions, and receive personalized recommendations. This personal touch makes the experience more intimate and tailored, which can lead to higher customer satisfaction and loyalty.

2. Customized Sales Experience

In direct selling, every customer interaction should be tailored to their needs and preferences. By taking the time to understand what the customer is looking for, you can offer recommendations that are specific to their situation, increasing the likelihood of making a sale. This level of customization makes the customer feel valued and heard.

[26] https://www.zendesk.com/blog/direct-selling/

For instance, a home-based business selling kitchen gadgets might ask customers about their cooking habits before suggesting products. A customer who enjoys baking might be shown items that help with precision and efficiency in the kitchen, while a customer who values convenience might be introduced to time-saving tools.

3. Building Trust

Direct selling relies heavily on building trust between the salesperson and the customer. Establishing credibility through honest, transparent communication is essential. By consistently providing value and being responsive to the customer's needs, direct sellers can foster long-term relationships that lead to repeat business and referrals.

For example, in the niche market of wellness products, direct sellers often rely on personal testimonials and word-of-mouth to build trust. By sharing their own positive experiences with the products and being available to answer questions, they establish a sense of trust that makes customers more likely to buy.

Best Fit: Direct selling is most effective in industries where personal interaction and relationship-building are key, such as in direct sales companies, home-based businesses, and niche markets where customers expect a customized and personal experience.

Transactional Selling

Transactional selling[27] is a straightforward, fast-paced technique that focuses on making quick sales without emphasizing long-term relationships or deep customer engagement. It's often used for lower-value, high-volume transactions where the goal is efficiency and speed rather than personalization. In this model, the emphasis is on moving

---

[27]https://secondnature.ai/what-is-transactional-selling-and-how-does-it-work/

the customer smoothly through the buying process with minimal friction.

1. Quick Sales

The primary goal of transactional selling is to close sales as quickly as possible. This involves streamlining the buying process and reducing the number of touchpoints between the customer and the final purchase. The faster and more efficiently the transaction can be completed, the better.

For example, in retail environments, transactional selling is often seen in the form of checkout counters or online shopping carts. The focus is on making the sale as fast and seamless as possible, with minimal barriers or extra steps.

2. Clear Offers

In transactional selling, offers and pricing need to be straightforward and easy to understand. Customers should be able to make a decision quickly without needing to engage in lengthy discussions or negotiations. Clear, transparent pricing and simple product descriptions help facilitate quick decision-making.

For instance, an online marketplace might offer a flash sale with clear discounts and limited-time offers. The pricing is displayed prominently, and the customer can quickly add the item to their cart and checkout without needing to spend time reviewing complex product details.

3. Minimized Interaction

Transactional selling often minimizes the level of personal interaction between the salesperson and the customer. Instead, the focus is on automating or streamlining the sales process to allow for higher volume and faster transactions. This approach works well in industries where customers already know what they want and don't need extensive consultations.

For example, in a fast-food restaurant, the transaction is quick, the interaction with the cashier is brief, and the emphasis is on efficiently moving customers through the line. The goal is to serve as many customers as possible in a short period of time without the need for personalized service.

Best Fit: Transactional selling is most effective in industries that rely on high-volume, low-value transactions, such as retail, fast-moving consumer goods, and online marketplaces. This technique is ideal for customers looking for convenience, speed, and clear offers without extensive engagement.

To sum things up, mastering a range of sales techniques is crucial for driving success in today's diverse and dynamic marketplace. From building trust and credibility through Referral Selling and Storytelling to leveraging personal interactions in Direct Selling and streamlining efficiency with Transactional Selling, each method has its unique strengths and applications. The key is understanding which technique to apply based on your audience, the product or service you're offering, and the overall sales environment.

By incorporating these approaches into your sales strategy, you equip yourself with the tools to engage customers more effectively, create lasting relationships, and drive higher conversions. Whether you're nurturing long-term clients or closing quick, high-volume transactions, the flexibility and depth of these techniques ensure you can adapt and thrive in any sales situation. Ultimately, the success of any sales team lies in their ability to adapt and innovate, applying the right techniques at the right time to meet both customer needs and business goals.

CHAPTER 5

Overcoming Sales Objections and Closing Deals

"Obstacles are those frightful things you see when you take your eyes off your goal."

– Henry Ford.

In the world of sales, objections are not obstacles to be feared but opportunities to be embraced. They signal that a prospect is engaged, curious, and on the cusp of making a decision but not yet convinced. Far from being a barrier, each objection is a chance to build trust, clarify doubts, and showcase the unique value of your product or service.

Mastering the art of overcoming sales objections requires more than just a script; it demands a deep understanding of both the logical and emotional factors that influence a buyer's decision-making process. This chapter explores successful sales professionals' techniques to transform objections into stepping stones toward closing deals. Whether it's navigating price concerns or addressing product comparisons, learning to view objections as opportunities rather than setbacks is key to turning prospects into satisfied customers.

The Nature of Sales Objections

Sales objections are an inevitable and natural part of the sales process. Rather than seeing them as obstacles, savvy sales professionals understand that objections are opportunities. They offer valuable insights into the customer's thought process, providing a chance to engage more deeply, uncover hidden concerns, and ultimately demonstrate the value of the product or service being offered. Embracing objections allows salespeople to build stronger, more trusting relationships with their prospects.

Why It's Important

Objections often reveal underlying gaps in understanding or confidence about a product or service. These gaps can be related to price, product features, implementation challenges, or even the perceived value of the offering. When addressed properly, these objections can be pivotal moments in the sales conversation. They provide an opportunity for the salesperson to clarify misunderstandings, reinforce the benefits of their product, and build the prospect's confidence in making a purchase decision. Successfully navigating objections strengthens the relationship between the salesperson and the customer, moving the prospect closer to saying "yes."

The Science

From a data-driven perspective, objections are often a positive sign of interest. Research shows that when prospects raise concerns, they are not necessarily rejecting the product but seeking clarification or reassurance. By analyzing common objections and understanding patterns in customer behavior, sales teams can refine their approaches and develop more effective responses. For example, if data indicates that price is a frequent concern, sales professionals can prepare detailed ROI analyses or case studies that preemptively address these concerns. This proactive approach increases close rates and enhances the overall customer experience.

The Art

While data provides a solid foundation, the art of handling objections lies in understanding and responding to the human side of the sales process. This involves empathy, active listening, and the ability to read non-verbal cues. Building rapport with the prospect is crucial; it allows the salesperson to address objections in a way that feels natural and supportive rather than confrontational. Storytelling is another powerful tool in this context; by sharing relevant anecdotes or case studies, salespeople can connect with prospects on an emotional level, helping them visualize the benefits of the product in their own lives. Understanding the psychology behind objections and responding with empathy fosters trust and demonstrates that the salesperson genuinely cares about the prospect's needs[28].

Examples of Handling Objections

Example 1: Price Concerns

Price is one of the most common objections in sales. When a prospect mentions that a competitor offers a cheaper product, the salesperson should acknowledge this concern while differentiating their offering. For example, "I understand that price is a critical factor. Many of our customers initially had the same concern, but they found that while our product may cost more upfront, the long-term ROI through reduced maintenance costs and improved efficiency far outweighs the initial investment." By coupling empathy with data on long-term value, the salesperson can help the prospect see the bigger picture.

Example 2: Learning Curve

In industries like software, a common objection is the learning curve associated with implementing a new system. A salesperson can address this by empathizing with the concern and providing evidence that others have successfully overcome it. For instance, "I understand that learning a new system can be daunting. One of our clients, who had similar concerns, found that our comprehensive onboarding process made the transition smoother than they expected, and within a

[28] https://www.tacresults.com/blog/empathy-helps-you-handle-objections/

few weeks, their team was fully up and running." This approach addresses the objection and builds rapport by sharing a success story that the prospect can relate to[29].

Effective objection handling is not just about overcoming barriers; it's about building trust and credibility with potential customers. When salespeople address objections transparently and knowledgeably, they convey a genuine interest in helping the prospect rather than merely pushing for a sale. This transparency fosters trust, which is crucial for converting prospects into customers.

By treating objections as feedback rather than roadblocks, sales professionals can gain deeper insights into their customers' needs and expectations. This perspective allows them to tailor their approach, provide relevant information, and build stronger relationships. Mastering the art and science of objection handling can transform objections from hurdles into opportunities for building trust, demonstrating value, and closing deals.

Overcoming Price Objections

Price objections are among the most common and challenging hurdles in sales. However, instead of viewing them as barriers, sales professionals can reframe these objections as opportunities to emphasize their product or service's unique value. Effectively addressing price objections is crucial for closing the deal and building customer confidence and long-term satisfaction. When handled correctly, these objections can be transformed into moments where the customer sees the true worth of the investment rather than just the cost.

---

[29] https://fastercapital.com/topics/storytelling-techniques-for-overcoming-objections.html

Why It's Important

Price is often the first and most significant barrier potential customers encounter during sales. However, objections regarding price typically stem from a lack of understanding of the product's value proposition. Customers may perceive the cost as too high because they haven't fully grasped how the product will benefit them in the long run. By balancing financial data with an emotional appeal, sales professionals can overcome this hurdle and instill confidence in the purchase decision. It's not just about justifying the cost; it's about helping the customer see the investment as a pathway to greater success.

The Science

Quantifying your product's value is a critical strategy in overcoming price objections. This can be done through ROI estimates, financial models, and case studies that illustrate the tangible benefits of the investment. Research indicates that customers respond positively to data-driven arguments, which can significantly influence their purchasing decisions. For instance, a study published in the Harvard Business Review highlights that providing clear context about pricing can help mitigate objections by illustrating the comprehensive value of your offerings compared to alternatives. When customers see hard numbers demonstrating how your product can save money, increase efficiency, or drive revenue, they are more likely to view the price as justified[30].

The Art

While data is essential, price is also an emotional decision for many customers. Crafting a narrative that positions the product as an investment in the customer's future growth can help justify its cost. A well-timed story can ease financial concerns and create a more relatable context for the price being discussed. Emotional connections are

---

[30] https://www.salesmate.io/blog/price-is-too-high/

powerful; when customers feel a connection to a brand or product, they are more likely to justify higher prices based on perceived value. For example, by telling a story about how another customer faced similar financial concerns but ultimately found great success with the product, you can help the prospect see beyond the immediate cost and focus on the potential rewards.

Examples of Addressing Price Objections

Example 1: ROI Calculator

When a prospect expresses concern about the price being too high, a salesperson can utilize an ROI calculator to show projected savings over time. For instance, if selling a high-end CRM system, the salesperson could input data specific to the prospect's business—such as current sales volume, conversion rates, and time spent on administrative tasks—to calculate how the CRM would lead to increased sales and efficiency. By detailing how the product will lead to cost reductions or increased revenue, the salesperson frames the purchase as a strategic investment rather than an expense, helping the customer see the long-term value.

Example 2: Daily Cost Breakdown

If a customer hesitates due to budget constraints, breaking down the product's cost into smaller increments can be an effective approach. For example, suppose a customer balks at a $365 annual subscription fee for a software service. In that case, the salesperson might reframe the conversation by saying, "For just $1 a day, you can have access to this powerful tool that will save you countless hours and help grow your business." This makes the investment seem more manageable and highlights the value of the product in relation to its daily cost.

Overcoming Objections Around Product Features

Feature objections arise when potential customers express doubts about whether a product can meet their specific needs. These objections are more than just barriers; they're opportunities to dive deeper into the customer's concerns and demonstrate how your product can be tailored to solve their unique challenges. Addressing these objections effectively is crucial because they often signal a need for more clarity and personalization. By aligning product features with the customer's pain points and goals, sales professionals can turn skepticism into satisfaction, paving the way for a successful sale.

Why It's Important

Understanding and overcoming feature objections is vital for several reasons:

- **Clarity and Personalization:** Feature objections often indicate that the customer needs more information or a clearer understanding of how the product can address their specific challenges. By responding to these objections with tailored explanations and examples, sales professionals can provide the clarity the customer needs to move forward confidently.
- **Building Trust:** Successfully addressing feature objections helps build trust between the salesperson and the prospect. When a salesperson takes the time to understand and respond to a customer's specific concerns, it demonstrates a commitment to their success. This trust is crucial for closing deals and fostering long-term relationships.
- **Informed Decision-Making:** Customers who receive clear, detailed information about how product features will benefit them are more likely to make informed purchasing decisions. This leads to higher satisfaction, reduced buyer's remorse, and increased loyalty.

The Science

To effectively counter feature objections, leveraging data-driven insights is essential. Here's how you can use the science of data to your advantage:

- **Customer Data:** Utilize analytics to understand how existing customers use your product and which features most benefit them. This evidence can be a powerful tool when addressing objections, as it shows the real-world application of your product. For instance, if a potential customer doubts the value of a particular feature, you can share data on how similar businesses have successfully utilized that feature to achieve their goals.

- **Usage Statistics:** Presenting concrete statistics can help demonstrate the effectiveness of specific features. For example, if a reporting tool in your software has been shown to reduce project delays by 30%, this statistic becomes a compelling piece of evidence that can help overcome skepticism. Data like this makes the benefits of your product tangible and difficult to dispute.

- **Case Studies:** Case studies are particularly effective in overcoming feature objections because they provide detailed examples of how your product has solved similar problems for other clients. By highlighting specific challenges faced by previous customers and demonstrating how your product features provided effective solutions, you can give prospects the reassurance they need.

The Art

While data is crucial, the art of overcoming objections lies in how you communicate and connect with the customer. Here's how to master this aspect:

- **Active Listening:** The first step in addressing feature objections is to listen actively to the customer's concerns. This means paying close attention without interrupting, allowing the customer to express their doubts or confusion fully. Active listening shows respect, builds rapport, and ensures that you fully understand the issue before offering a solution.

- **Tailored Responses:** Once you've understood the customer's concerns, tailor your response to address their specific situation. Sharing relatable success stories can be particularly effective. For example, if a customer is worried about a feature's complexity, you might recount how another client successfully integrated that feature into their workflow with minimal disruption. This personal touch can make your response more convincing and relevant.

- **Personalized Demos or Trials:** Offering personalized demos or free trials can significantly reduce hesitation. These hands-on experiences allow customers to see for themselves how your product fits into their daily operations. For example, if a prospect is unsure about how a particular feature will work with their existing systems, a tailored demo that walks them through the integration process can alleviate concerns and build confidence in your solution.

Examples of Overcoming Feature Objections

Example 1: Linking Features to Business Problems

One of the most effective ways to overcome feature objections is by directly linking the features to the prospect's business problems. For instance, if a customer is concerned about the effectiveness of a reporting tool, you could explain how it has helped other companies reduce project delays by 30%. This direct correlation between the feature and a tangible business outcome makes the value of the feature clear and relevant. It shifts the conversation from "What does this feature do?" to "How will this feature solve my problem?"—which is ultimately what the customer cares about.

Example 2: Offering Personalized Experiences

Another powerful technique is offering personalized experiences, such as demos or trials, that address the customer's specific concerns. For example, if a prospect is hesitant about adopting your software due to uncertainty about its fit within their existing processes, arranging a personalized demo that showcases how the product integrates seamlessly into their workflow can be highly effective. This practical demonstration allows the customer to see the product in action, alleviates fears about compatibility or complexity, and builds confidence in your solution.

By addressing feature objections with science and art—leveraging data to provide evidence while communicating with empathy and personalization—sales professionals can turn potential deal-breakers into deal-closers. Understanding the root of the objection, providing clear and relevant information, and offering tailored solutions are key to overcoming these hurdles and moving the sales process forward.

Competitor Comparisons

Competitor comparisons are a strategic tool that allows businesses to highlight their product's unique strengths while maintaining a respectful and factual approach toward competitors. This method is essential for effectively positioning your product in a competitive landscape. When done correctly, competitor comparisons help differentiate your product and build credibility with potential customers, guiding them toward a more informed purchasing decision.

Why It's Important

Understanding the significance of competitor comparisons involves several key factors:

- **Customer Decision-Making:** In today's information-rich environment, customers often conduct extensive research and engage in comparative analysis before making a purchasing decision. They want to know how different products stack up against each other in terms of features, pricing, and overall value. A well-articulated comparison can help customers understand why your product may best fit their needs, especially if they are on the fence or leaning toward a competitor.

- **Highlighting Differentiators:** Competitor comparisons provide an opportunity to showcase your product's unique features and advantages. By presenting these differentiators clearly and factually, you can communicate your product's value proposition without resorting to negative tactics that could alienate potential customers. For example, highlighting these aspects can make your offering stand out if your product offers a key feature that competitors lack or if your service includes additional benefits at no extra cost.

- **Building Credibility:** A balanced and respectful approach to competitor comparisons fosters trust and credibility. It shows prospects that you respect their ability to make informed choices and that you are confident in your offering. Instead of undermining competitors with negative comparisons, you position your product as a superior choice based on objective criteria. This approach can be particularly effective in building long-term relationships with customers who value transparency and integrity.

The Science

To effectively showcase your product's strengths, relying on objective, data-backed insights is important. This scientific approach ensures that your comparisons are credible and persuasive.

- **Feature Comparisons:** Use specific metrics to compare features. For instance, provide statistics that quantify this advantage if your product offers superior customer support response times. For example, "Our average response time is under two hours, compared to the industry standard of four hours." This type of comparison highlights your product's strengths and provides concrete data that prospects can trust.

- **Pricing Models:** Analyze and present how your pricing structure compares favorably against competitors. This might involve highlighting cost-saving benefits, such as bundled services or lower total cost of ownership over time. For example, "While our upfront costs may be higher, our solution includes maintenance and support, which saves you money in the long run compared to Competitor X's additional fees."

- **Customer Support:** Share customer satisfaction rates, support response times, or service availability data to illustrate how your service outperforms others in the market. For instance, "Our customer satisfaction rate is 95%, with a dedicated support team available 24/7, ensuring that any issues are resolved promptly."

- **SWOT Analysis:** Conduct a SWOT analysis (Strengths, Weaknesses, Opportunities, Threats) for both your product and competitors. This structured approach helps identify areas where you excel and where competitors may fall short. For example, if a competitor's product is known for its complexity, you could emphasize the user-friendliness of your solution as a key strength [31] [32].

The Art

While data is critical, the art of competitor comparisons lies in how you communicate these insights. The way you present this information can significantly impact how the prospect receives it.

- **Respectful Positioning:** Frame your comparisons in a way that acknowledges competitors' strengths while clearly articulating why your product is a better fit for the prospect's specific needs. For example, you might say, "While Competitor A offers a robust platform, our solution is designed for businesses that prioritize ease of use and quick implementation, which can save your team valuable time."

- **Balanced Tone:** Maintain a balanced tone throughout your discussions. Highlight what you offer without unnecessarily

---

[31] https://www.bdc.ca/en/articles-tools/marketing-sales-export/marketing/how-evaluate-competition

[32] https://blog.hubspot.com/marketing/competitive-analysis-kit

undermining the competition. This approach enhances your professionalism and appeal. For example, "Competitor B has a strong presence in the market, but our focus on personalized customer service sets us apart, providing you with tailored support that large companies may not offer."

- **Customer Testimonials:** Leverage customer testimonials to provide real-world examples of how clients have benefited from switching to your product after initially choosing a competitor. This narrative can resonate deeply with prospects who may be facing similar dilemmas. For instance, "One of our clients initially chose Competitor C but found their platform too rigid for their needs. After switching to our solution, they experienced a 40% increase in productivity within just three months[33] [34]."

Examples of Effective Competitor Comparisons

Example 1: Highlighting Key Differentiators

If your product has a notable advantage in a specific area, such as customer service response times, you can make this a focal point in your comparison. For instance, "While [Competitor A] provides solid services, our average response time is under two hours compared to their four-hour standard. This means you get faster resolutions when issues arise, minimizing downtime and keeping your operations running smoothly." This type of comparison directly addresses a potential pain point for the prospect and positions your product as the superior choice.

---

33 https://www.linkedin.com/advice/1/what-some-best-practices-conducting-competitor

34 https://www.bigcommerce.com/blog/how-perform-competitive-analysis/

Example 2: Utilizing Customer Stories

Customer stories are powerful tools in competitor comparisons because they provide relatable, real-world examples of your product's benefits. For example, "One of our clients initially chose [Competitor B] but faced challenges with integration that led to project delays. After switching to our solution, they reported a 40% increase in efficiency within just three months, with a seamless integration process that met all their requirements." This highlights the practical advantages of your product and builds an emotional connection with the prospect, as they can see themselves in the success story.

Advanced Negotiation Techniques Using Buyer Psychology

Effective negotiation is both an art and a science, requiring a deep understanding of buyer psychology. By recognizing common decision-making patterns and leveraging psychological principles, sales professionals can influence the conversation to build trust and ultimately close deals. Techniques such as anchoring, scarcity, and reciprocity can be powerful tools in guiding the buyer toward a favorable outcome for both parties. When used with finesse and emotional intelligence, these strategies enhance the negotiation process and create long-lasting relationships based on trust and mutual benefit.

Why It's Important

Incorporating buyer psychology into negotiation strategies is crucial for several reasons:

- **Guiding Decision-Making:** Understanding how buyers make decisions allows sales professionals to shape the conversation in a way that leads to mutually beneficial outcomes. By tapping into the underlying psychological drivers of decision-making, salespeople can position their offers in a way that resonates more deeply with the buyer's needs and desires.

- **Building Trust:** Applying psychological principles with finesse and emotional intelligence helps create a sense of trust and rapport. When buyers feel understood and respected, they are more likely to be receptive to the negotiation process and open to finding a solution that works for both parties.

- **Closing Deals:** Effectively using buyer psychology in negotiations increases the likelihood of closing deals. By addressing the buyer's underlying motivations and concerns, sales professionals can remove obstacles to agreement and make the decision to purchase feel like a natural and positive choice.

The Science

Behavioral economics provides insights into how principles like loss aversion, reciprocity, and anchoring can influence buyer behavior. These principles are grounded in research and can be applied strategically in negotiations to guide buyer decisions.

- **Loss Aversion:** People tend to strongly prefer avoiding losses over acquiring gains. This principle can be leveraged by highlighting the potential downsides of not making a purchase or the benefits the buyer stands to lose by not acting now. For example, a salesperson might emphasize how delaying the decision could result in missing out on a limited-time discount or losing a competitive edge by not implementing the solution promptly. By framing the offer in terms of what the buyer could lose rather than just what they could gain, the salesperson can create a stronger incentive to close the deal.

- **Reciprocity:** The human tendency to respond to a positive action with another positive action can be harnessed in negotiations by providing value upfront. For instance, offering a free trial, complimentary consultation, or valuable industry insights makes the buyer more inclined to reciprocate by making a purchase. This principle works because it taps into a fundamental social norm—when someone does something for us, we feel a natural urge to return the favor.

- **Anchoring:** Anchoring is a cognitive bias that causes people to rely heavily on the first piece of information they receive when making decisions. In negotiations, presenting a high-value offer first, such as a comprehensive package with additional features or services, sets a high anchor point. This makes the standard offer appear more affordable and attractive by comparison. For example, if the initial proposal is for a premium package priced at $10,000, the next offer at $7,500 may seem like a better deal, even if it was originally the target price.

The Art

While science provides the foundation, the art of applying these principles lies in the execution. The effectiveness of psychological strategies in negotiation depends on how they are implemented.

- **Emotional Intelligence:** Sales professionals must use emotional intelligence to read the room and adjust their tone, pacing, and approach accordingly. This means being attuned to the buyer's emotional state, body language, and verbal cues and responding in a way that creates a sense of trust and rapport. For example, if a buyer seems hesitant or anxious, a soft, reassuring tone and a slower pace can help ease their concerns and make them more comfortable with the negotiation.

- **Subtlety:** Applying psychological principles with finesse is key to successful negotiation. Overt manipulation or pressure tactics can backfire, damaging the relationship and making the buyer less likely to agree to a deal. Instead, these principles should be used to gently guide the conversation in a way that feels organic and persuasive—for instance, creating a sense of scarcity by mentioning that "we only have a few units left at this price" should be done casually, without making the buyer feel pressured.

- **Flexibility:** Skilled negotiators are able to adapt their approach based on the buyer's reactions and feedback. This requires staying flexible and open to adjusting the strategy as needed to achieve the desired outcome. For example, suppose a buyer pushes back on price. In that case, the salesperson might pivot to emphasize the long-term value and ROI of the product rather than sticking rigidly to the initial offer.

Examples of Advanced Negotiation Techniques Using Buyer Psychology

Example 1: Anchoring

Anchoring is an effective technique in negotiations where setting the right reference point can make your offer more attractive. For example, you create a high anchor point when presenting a high-value offer—such as a comprehensive package with additional features or premium services. This makes subsequent offers appear more reasonable by comparison. For instance, "Our premium package includes X, Y, and Z for $10,000, but if you're looking for something more cost-effective, we can offer the standard package at $7,500." Doing so makes the standard offer feel like a bargain, increasing the likelihood of acceptance.

Example 2: Scarcity

Creating a sense of scarcity is another powerful psychological technique that can motivate buyers to act quickly. By subtly emphasizing that an offer is time-limited or that only a few units are left, you can create urgency without applying overt pressure. For example, "We only have a limited number of licenses available at this discounted rate, and once they're gone, the price will go back up." This approach allows the buyer to feel in control of their decision while still encouraging them to act swiftly to avoid missing out on a valuable opportunity.

The "Feel, Felt, Found" Method for Handling Objections

The "Feel, Felt, Found" method is a classic and powerful technique for handling objections in sales, combining empathy with the persuasive power of social proof. This approach helps sales professionals address customer concerns in a validating and reassuring way. By acknowledging the customer's feelings, sharing that others have experienced similar doubts, and demonstrating how those doubts were resolved, the "Feel, Felt, Found" method can transform objections into opportunities for deeper connection and trust, ultimately guiding the customer toward a positive purchasing decision.

Why It's Important

Understanding the significance of the "Feel, Felt, Found" method involves recognizing its psychological underpinnings:

- **Validation of Emotions:** At the core of this method is the validation of the customer's emotions. By acknowledging how the customer feels, sales professionals build rapport and trust. When customers feel understood and heard, they are more likely to engage positively in the conversation. This emotional connection is crucial for moving past objections and toward resolution.

- **Social Proof:** The "Felt" and "Found" components of the method leverage the principle of social proof, a psychological concept that suggests the actions and experiences of others influence people. When a salesperson shares that others had similar concerns and then found value in the product, it reassures the customer that their doubts are normal and that the product can meet their needs. This approach can significantly sway a customer's decision-making process by providing credible, relatable examples of success.

- **Effective Objection Handling:** The "Feel, Felt, Found" method provides a structured and empathetic way to address objections without alienating the customer. It guides them from their initial hesitation to a place of reassurance and confidence in their decision to purchase. This method is particularly effective because it doesn't dismiss the customer's concerns but instead acknowledges and addresses them in a constructive way.

The Science

Principles from psychology and behavioral economics support the effectiveness of the "Feel, Felt, Found" method:

- **Empathy and Trust:** Research shows that expressing empathy can increase trust between individuals. When salespeople demonstrate understanding through the "Feel" component, they foster a connection that makes customers more receptive to further dialogue. This is particularly important in sales, where trust is a key factor in closing deals.

- **Social Proof:** The concept of social proof, as outlined by Robert Cialdini in his work on influence, suggests that individuals look to the behavior of others when making decisions. By sharing stories of how others felt similarly yet found value in your product, you provide a compelling reason for the prospect to reconsider their objection. This technique taps into the human tendency to follow the lead of others, especially in situations of uncertainty.

- **Cognitive Dissonance:** When customers hear that others initially felt the same way but later found satisfaction with your product, it can create cognitive dissonance—a psychological state where a person experiences discomfort due to holding conflicting beliefs. In this case, the customer's objection may conflict with the positive outcomes experienced by others. This dissonance can prompt the customer to re-evaluate their stance, potentially leading them to align their beliefs with the positive experiences shared by the salesperson.

The Art

The art of using the "Feel, Felt, Found" method lies in its delivery:

- **Genuine Tone:** The effectiveness of this method depends largely on the sincerity of the delivery. Sales professionals must communicate with a genuine and empathetic tone. A rehearsed or insincere delivery can come across as patronizing and may increase resistance rather than alleviate it. However, this method can make the customer feel truly understood and respected when done authentically.

- **Personal Connection:** To enhance the impact of the "Feel, Felt, Found" method, use personal stories or relatable examples that create an emotional connection with the prospect. This helps reinforce the idea that they are not alone in their feelings and encourages them to open up about their concerns. For example, sharing a story about a similar client who faced the same objections but found success with the product can make the conversation more relatable and persuasive.

- **Tailored Responses:** The effectiveness of the "Feel, Felt, Found" method also depends on tailoring your responses to the specific objections raised by the customer. This customization demonstrates active listening and reinforces that you genuinely care about addressing their unique needs. For instance, if a customer is concerned about the complexity of a feature, the salesperson can share a story of a client who had similar concerns but found that the learning curve was manageable and ultimately beneficial.

Examples of Using the "Feel, Felt, Found" Method

Example 1: Price Objection

When a customer expresses concern about the price, a salesperson might respond with the "Feel, Felt, Found" method like this:

"I understand how you feel about the price; it's a significant investment. Many of our clients felt the same way initially, especially when comparing costs with other options. However, what they found was that the investment paid off significantly when they saw improvements in efficiency and productivity, which more than justified the upfront cost."

This approach not only acknowledges the customer's concern but also shifts the focus to the product's long-term value.

Example 2: Personal Story

Sharing a personal anecdote can also be powerful:

"When I first encountered this product, I had reservations, too. I felt unsure about its effectiveness until I saw firsthand how it transformed my workflow. What I found was that it not only met but exceeded my expectations, making my job easier and more efficient."

This personal touch can resonate with the customer, as it shows that the salesperson has also navigated similar concerns and found value in the product.

Closing the Deal

Closing the deal is the pinnacle of the sales process, where interest is transformed into action, and a prospect becomes a customer. This crucial phase requires a blend of science and art, combining data-driven strategies with a nuanced understanding of buyer psychology. Recognizing the right moment and employing the appropriate closing techniques are key to successfully converting prospects, ensuring customer satisfaction, and fostering long-term relationships.

Why It's Important

Closing is a critical phase in the sales process for several reasons:

- **Conversion of Interest:** The close is the final step in converting a prospect's interest into a commitment. This transition is vital for achieving sales targets, driving revenue, and ensuring the success of the sales process. Even the most promising leads can fall through without a successful close, resulting in lost opportunities.

- **Identifying Readiness:** Understanding when a buyer is ready to close is crucial for timing the approach correctly. Recognizing the buyer's emotional state and readiness to make a decision allows sales professionals to tailor their closing technique, ensuring that it aligns with the buyer's mindset and increases the likelihood of a positive outcome.

- **Building Long-Term Relationships:** A well-executed close does more than secure a sale; it enhances customer satisfaction and loyalty. By closing in a natural and supportive way, sales professionals can lay the groundwork for future business opportunities and referrals, turning a one-time transaction into a long-term relationship.

The Science

Closing techniques can be informed by recognizing buying signals and utilizing data-driven strategies. Understanding the science behind closing helps sales professionals make informed decisions about when and how to move forward.

- **Buying Signals:** Research indicates that buyers often exhibit specific behaviors or verbal cues that signal their readiness to purchase. These signals can include asking detailed questions about implementation, requesting pricing information, expressing enthusiasm about the product, or discussing potential timelines. Recognizing these signals allows sales professionals to choose the appropriate closing strategy and move forward with confidence.

- **Closing Strategies:** Different situations call for different closing techniques. Here are some of the most effective strategies:

    - **Trial Close:** This method involves gauging interest by asking questions that assume a positive response. For example, "Shall we schedule the installation for next week?" or "Does this solution meet all your needs so far?" This technique helps assess readiness without putting undue pressure on the buyer and can also reveal any remaining objections that need to be addressed before moving forward.

    - **Assumptive Close:** This approach involves acting as if the buyer has already decided to purchase. By framing questions or statements in this way, salespeople can create momentum toward closing. For instance, saying, "I'll prepare the contract for you to review this afternoon," subtly nudges the buyer toward finalizing the deal.

- **Alternative Close:** Presenting options can help buyers feel in control of their decision. For example, "Would you prefer the standard package or the premium option with additional support?" This method encourages decision-making without forcing a choice, making the buyer feel more comfortable and empowered.

The Art

The art of closing lies in emotional intelligence and the ability to read the buyer's emotional state. While science provides a foundation, it's the art of closing that ensures the process feels smooth and natural.

- **Reading the Room:** Skilled sales professionals must be adept at interpreting buyers' non-verbal cues and emotional signals. This includes observing body language, tone of voice, and overall demeanor to gauge comfort levels. For instance, if a buyer seems hesitant or nervous, a more gentle approach may be necessary, whereas enthusiasm might call for a more direct close.

- **Guiding Conversations:** Closing should feel like a natural progression of the conversation rather than a forced conclusion. By maintaining an open dialogue and addressing any lingering concerns, salespeople can facilitate a smoother transition to closing. For example, revisiting key points that resonated with the buyer earlier in the conversation can help reinforce the value proposition and lead naturally into the close.

- **Emotional Connection:** Building rapport throughout the sales process enhances trust, making it easier for buyers to commit. Acknowledging their emotions—such as excitement or apprehension—can help create a supportive environment conducive to closing. For example, saying, "I can see how excited you are about this solution, and I think it's a perfect fit for your needs," helps to validate their feelings and encourages them to move forward.

Examples of Effective Closing Techniques

Example 1: Assumptive Close

When a buyer begins asking detailed questions about logistics or implementation, it signals readiness. A salesperson might respond with, "Shall we schedule the installation for next week?" This approach assumes interest and encourages commitment by subtly moving the conversation toward action. The assumptive close is effective because it minimizes the perceived risk of the decision, making the buyer feel as though the next steps are a natural progression.

Example 2: Alternative Close

Presenting choices can empower buyers by giving them a sense of control over the decision. For example, "Would you prefer our standard package, or would you like to explore our premium option with additional support?" This technique helps steer the buyer toward making a decision while allowing them to feel in control. By offering alternatives, the salesperson creates a scenario where the buyer is more focused on which option to choose rather than whether to choose at all.

Persistence and Adaptability

Sales success is as much about persistence as it is about adaptability. Knowing when to push forward and when to pull back is essential in building long-term relationships with customers. The ability to maintain engagement through multiple touchpoints while adjusting your approach based on customer cues is key to keeping prospects interested without overwhelming them.

Why It's Important

Sales often require several interactions before a deal is closed, making persistence crucial. However, it's not just about the number of touchpoints but about the quality and timing of those interactions. The ability to adapt your strategy based on the customer's signals helps maintain a balance between being persistent and being considerate of their decision-making process.

- **The Science:** Research indicates that closing a deal typically takes five to seven touchpoints. Utilizing CRM systems can help track these interactions, ensuring timely and relevant follow-up. By monitoring customer engagement, sales professionals can strategically plan their next steps, increasing the likelihood of a successful close.

- **The Art:** Persistence must be paired with adaptability to be effective. Knowing when to give the customer space and when to re-engage requires a keen understanding of their signals. For example, if a customer seems hesitant, offering a free trial or additional information can help them feel more confident in their decision. This approach builds trust and respect, which are essential for long-term customer relationships.

By mastering the balance between persistence and adaptability, sales professionals can navigate the complexities of the sales process with greater ease, ultimately leading to more successful and sustainable outcomes.

CHAPTER 6

Measuring Sales Success and Driving Continuous Improvement

"Without data, you're just another person with an opinion."

– W. Edwards Deming

In today's fiercely competitive sales environment, true success is about more than just meeting sales targets; it's about creating a sustainable, adaptive system that continuously evolves. Measuring sales success requires more than a superficial glance at revenue figures; it calls for a data-driven approach that provides deep insights into every aspect of your sales strategy. By leveraging the right tools and techniques, sales professionals can transform raw data into actionable insights that drive continuous improvement.

This chapter will explore how data visualization tools like Tableau can present sales data in compelling, interactive ways, helping sales teams track performance and make informed decisions. We'll also dive into the principles of continuous process improvement, using methodologies like Six Sigma, tailored specifically for sales environments. In addition, we'll examine the importance of tracking Key Performance Indicators (KPIs) to guide business sales leaders in maintaining a clear focus on what truly drives growth.

The Role of Data Visualization in Sales

In today's data-driven sales environment, the ability to translate vast amounts of information into actionable insights is critical for success. Data visualization tools, such as Tableau, have become transformative assets that enable sales teams to create interactive, shareable dashboards, effectively bringing sales metrics to life.

By leveraging visual representations of data, sales leaders can more readily identify trends, monitor performance against goals, and pinpoint potential bottlenecks or opportunities. These visual tools not only simplify complex data but also empower teams to make informed, timely decisions.

Benefits of Data Visualization in Sales

Data visualization enhances decision-making processes by offering clarity and enabling quicker responses to changes in the market. Here are some key benefits[35]:

- **Discover Hidden Patterns:** Data visualization tools allow sales teams to identify patterns and trends that might otherwise go unnoticed quickly. For example, a sales dashboard can reveal shifts in customer preferences or product performance over time, enabling teams to adjust strategies accordingly. This could mean identifying a surge in demand for a particular product in a specific region or recognizing that a certain sales approach is consistently underperforming.

- **Faster Response Time:** With real-time insights, sales teams can optimize their processes and improve collaboration with other departments, such as marketing. The ability to view data in real-time ensures that both sales and marketing teams are

---

[35]https://www.itconvergence.com/blog/benefits-of-data-visualization-for-sales-teams/

aligned on goals and can make quick, informed decisions to seize opportunities or address challenges. For instance, if a marketing campaign is driving significant traffic but not converting to sales, the team can adjust messaging or offers to increase effectiveness[36].

- **Analyze Data from Multiple Sources:** Data visualization tools like Tableau can integrate information from various platforms, such as CRM systems, marketing automation tools, and financial software, to provide a unified view of sales and marketing performance. This holistic perspective allows teams to analyze how different factors, such as customer engagement, lead generation, and sales closures, work together to drive business outcomes[37].

- **Track and Measure KPIs:** Visualizing key performance indicators (KPIs) allows sales leaders to quickly assess team performance and make data-driven decisions about resource allocation and strategy adjustments. For example, a dashboard displaying KPIs like sales revenue, conversion rates, and customer acquisition costs can help leaders pinpoint areas where performance is lagging and develop targeted improvement strategies.

- **Improve Collaboration:** Role-based dashboards can be tailored to present relevant information to specific team members, improving communication and ensuring that everyone interprets the data consistently. This shared understanding fosters collaboration within the sales team and across departments, ensuring that everyone is working towards the same objectives with the same data.

---

36 https://www.intelemark.com/blog/data-visualization-in-b2b-sales/
37 https://blog.exactbuyer.com/post/benefits-data-visualization-sales

- **Increase Productivity:** Companies that utilize data visualization tools report significantly higher efficiency in accessing timely information compared to those relying solely on traditional reporting methods. Sales personnel spend less time analyzing data and more time focusing on selling activities. For example, instead of sifting through spreadsheets, a sales rep can quickly pull up a dashboard to see how their performance compares to targets and adjust their strategy accordingly[38].

For example, a Tableau dashboard can be configured to display real-time metrics such as sales revenue, conversion rates, and customer acquisition costs. The ability to drill down into specifics—like individual salesperson performance or geographic trends—equips sales leaders with the insights necessary to make strategic decisions that drive growth.

Continuous Process Improvement Using Six Sigma Techniques

While Six Sigma methodologies are traditionally associated with manufacturing, their principles have been effectively adapted for use in sales environments. Six Sigma focuses on reducing variability and improving efficiency, and when applied to sales, it can lead to significant performance improvements. By continuously refining sales processes, organizations can increase productivity, enhance customer satisfaction, and ultimately drive revenue growth.

Applying the DMAIC Framework

The DMAIC (Define, Measure, Analyze, Improve, Control) framework from Six Sigma is particularly useful for evaluating and refining sales processes:

---

[38] https://www.revenue.io/inside-sales-glossary/what-is-sales-data-visualization

- **Define:** Clearly outline the objectives of the improvement initiative. This could involve enhancing conversion rates, shortening the sales cycle, or improving lead quality. The more specific the goal, the easier it will be to track progress and measure success. For example, a company may define its objective as reducing the average sales cycle from 60 days to 45 days.

- **Measure:** Utilize key performance indicators (KPIs) to collect data and establish baseline metrics. This step is essential for understanding the current performance of the sales team and identifying areas that require improvement. Sales leaders might track metrics like average deal size, time to close, or lead-to-customer conversion rates.

- **Analyze:** In this phase, teams analyze the data to identify the root causes of inefficiencies or performance gaps. For example, if conversion rates are lower than expected, the analysis might reveal that leads are not being followed up with promptly or that sales reps lack adequate training on a new product.

- **Improve:** Based on the insights gathered during the analysis phase, teams implement changes to optimize sales processes. These changes might involve retraining the sales team, automating certain tasks, or refining the sales pitch to better align with customer needs.

- **Control:** Once improvements have been made, it's essential to monitor the results to ensure that the changes are having the desired effect and that performance improvements are sustained over time. This could involve setting up regular check-ins or dashboards to using track progress against the newly established KPIs[39] [40].

Benefits of Six Sigma in Sales

Organizations that have successfully integrated Six Sigma into their sales processes often report enhanced customer satisfaction and increased revenue growth. For example, companies like 3M and Johnson & Johnson have utilized these methodologies to streamline their sales operations and improve overall effectiveness.

By adopting a Six Sigma mindset within their sales teams, leaders can ensure continuous refinement of processes and strategies. This approach not only leads to better sales performance but also fosters a more agile organization capable of responding swiftly to market changes. For example, if market trends shift and a company needs to reallocate resources to meet new demands, Six Sigma methodologies provide a structured framework for making those adjustments effectively and efficiently.

Incorporating continuous process improvement into the sales strategy allows organizations to stay competitive in an ever-evolving marketplace. By focusing on both the science of data and the art of process refinement, sales leaders can build a culture of constant improvement that drives long-term success.

---

[39] https://rcm.ac.in/six-sigma-in-sales-and-marketing-enhancing-competitiveness/

[40] https://www.simplilearn.com/tutorials/tableau-tutorial/tableau-dashboard-examples

Tools for Measuring Sales Success

In the modern business landscape, measuring sales success has advanced far beyond traditional spreadsheets. Interactive tools like Tableau offer dynamic platforms that allow sales teams to visualize performance data in real-time, transforming raw numbers into actionable insights. These tools not only enhance data accessibility but also enable informed decision-making by presenting complex information in an easily digestible format. By leveraging these cutting-edge tools, sales teams can stay agile, making data-driven adjustments to their strategies with confidence and precision.

The Importance of Interactive Dashboards

Interactive dashboards are the backbone of modern sales analytics, providing robust, shareable insights into sales performance. Tools like Tableau allow sales leaders to build dashboards that consolidate critical data into a visually appealing, real-time interface. These dashboards offer more than just a snapshot of performance; they provide an in-depth look into various facets of the sales process, enabling teams to drill down into specific areas that need attention or optimization.

For example, a well-designed Tableau dashboard might feature the following:

- **Sales Performance Tracking:** Visualizations that display key metrics such as revenue growth, conversion rates, and customer acquisition costs. These metrics allow teams to monitor progress against targets and identify whether they are on track to meet or exceed their goals.

- **Customer Insights:** Dashboards can offer detailed analysis of customer behavior, segmentation, and buying patterns, allowing sales teams to tailor their strategies to meet the unique needs of different customer groups. For example, insights into which demographics are most responsive to certain products can guide targeted sales efforts.

- **Product Performance Monitoring:** Dashboards can also help sales leaders understand which products or services are driving the most revenue, as well as those that are underperforming. This information enables strategic adjustments, such as reallocating resources to promote high-demand products or rethinking sales approaches for slower-moving inventory.

Interactive dashboards enable sales teams to assess performance in real-time and respond quickly to emerging trends. For instance, the Tableau Sales Performance Tracker Dashboard provides a comprehensive overview of sales and margin performance across products and customer segments, helping sales leaders make data-driven adjustments to their strategies[41].

Key Performance Indicators (KPIs) for Sales Leaders

Key Performance Indicators (KPIs) are essential metrics that sales leaders use to track performance and guide strategic decision-making. By monitoring the right KPIs, sales teams can identify strengths, address weaknesses, and optimize their approach to meet business objectives. Below are some of the most critical KPIs that businesses should monitor to gauge their sales success:

Sales Revenue

Sales revenue is the most fundamental KPI for any sales organization. It measures the total income generated from sales over a specific period, providing a clear indication of whether sales efforts are translating into tangible business growth. Monitoring sales revenue helps leaders assess the overall effectiveness of their sales strategies and determine whether the team is on track to meet its goals. For example,

---

[41]https://www.phdata.io/blog/tableau-sales-performance-tracker-dashboard/

tracking monthly or quarterly revenue trends can highlight seasonal patterns or reveal the success of recent marketing campaigns.

Customer Acquisition Cost (CAC)

Customer Acquisition Cost (CAC) calculates the average cost incurred to acquire a new customer. It includes all marketing, sales, and related expenses needed to convert a lead into a paying customer. Keeping CAC low is crucial for maximizing return on investment (ROI) and improving profitability. A rising CAC may indicate inefficiencies in the sales funnel, suggesting the need for process improvements or better alignment between sales and marketing efforts. By comparing CAC against lifetime customer value (LTV), sales teams can also determine whether they are acquiring customers profitably.

Conversion Rate

The conversion rate is a vital KPI that measures the percentage of leads that convert into paying customers. A high conversion rate suggests an effective sales process, while a low conversion rate may indicate bottlenecks or issues in the sales funnel. Monitoring conversion rates can help sales leaders identify areas where the team excels and where improvements are needed. For example, if leads consistently drop off during product demonstrations, it might indicate the need for better training or more refined sales presentations. Enhancing conversion rates can have a direct impact on revenue growth, making this an essential metric to track closely.

Average Deal Size

Average deal size measures the average value of each closed sale and helps sales leaders assess how well the team is capitalizing on opportunities to maximize revenue. Tracking this KPI allows sales teams to identify opportunities for upselling or cross-selling, which can significantly boost overall sales performance. For instance, if the average deal size begins to shrink, it may suggest that customers are opting for lower-tier products or services, signaling the need for more aggressive upselling strategies.

Sales Success Index (SSI)

The **Sales Success Index (SSI)** is a powerful, versatile metric designed to provide sales leaders with a comprehensive understanding of their team's performance. By incorporating key factors like total sales, deal size, margin, customer acquisition cost, conversion rate, and strategic importance, the SSI offers a holistic view of not just short-term results but also long-term strategic impact. This makes it a valuable tool for assessing both the quantity and quality of sales efforts. The SSI is important because it enables leaders to identify strengths and areas for improvement across all stages of the sales process, ensuring that sales strategies are aligned with business goals, profitability, and customer acquisition efficiency.

The SSI should be used regularly to track progress—ideally on a monthly or quarterly basis—depending on the sales cycle of your industry. It provides consistent insights into performance trends over time, allowing leaders to make informed adjustments to strategy. One of its most significant advantages is its flexibility: the SSI can be applied across any industry and works equally well for teams selling products or services. Whether you're leading a B2B technology firm, a retail business, or a healthcare services team, the SSI provides a reliable and standardized way to measure, compare, and improve sales outcomes across diverse markets and industries.

Creating a formula to measure the overall success of a sales team needed to include key variables that impact both short-term results and long-term strategic goals. Here's a breakdown of how you could create such a formula, combining both quantitative and qualitative factors:

$$\text{SSI} = \frac{(\text{Total Sales} \times \text{Average Deal Size} \times \text{Margin})}{\text{Customer Acquisition Cost (CAC)}} \times \text{Conversion rate} \times \text{Strategic Importance Weight}$$

In this formula:

- **Total Sales** = Number of deals closed
- **Avg. Deal Size** = Average value of each deal
- **Margin** = Profit margin on sales (as a percentage)

- **Customer Acquisition Cost (CAC)** = Cost of acquiring a new customer
- **Conversion Rate** = Percentage of leads converted into customers
- **Strategic Importance Weight** = Importance of each deal to the company's long-term strategy (scale of 0-1)

Explanation of the Variables:

- **Total Sales:** This represents the number of deals successfully closed by the sales team within a specific period. It serves as a fundamental indicator of overall performance, showing how productive the team is.

- **Average Deal Size:** The average value of each sale, recognizing that not all deals contribute equally. Larger deals bring in more revenue and often require more sophisticated strategies, so their size is an important factor.

- **Margin:** This refers to the profit margin on each sale. While a team may close many deals, profitability is what ultimately matters. Including margin ensures that the formula accounts for the actual financial value of the sales being made.

- **Customer Acquisition Cost (CAC):** This is the average cost incurred to acquire each new customer. Ideally, the team should aim to minimize CAC, making sure they are achieving sales efficiently without overspending on lead generation.

- **Conversion Rate:** This variable measures the percentage of leads converted into paying customers. A higher conversion rate indicates that the sales process is effective and efficient at moving leads through the funnel.

- **Strategic Importance Weight:** Some deals carry more weight in terms of long-term business strategy, such as breaking into new markets or landing a high-value customer. This variable assigns a score (on a scale of 0-1) to each deal based on its strategic significance to the company's future.

Breaking Down the Formula:

- **Profitability Component:** The initial part of the formula— $\frac{\text{Total Sales x Average Deal Size x Margin}}{\text{CAC}}$ — calculates the overall revenue impact relative to the cost of acquiring new customers. This ensures profitability is weighed against customer acquisition efficiency.

- **Sales Efficiency:** By multiplying the result by the **Conversion Rate**, the formula incorporates a measure of efficiency. Teams that convert a higher percentage of leads into paying customers are rewarded with a higher score.

- **Strategic Weighting:** Finally, multiplying by the **Strategic Importance Weight** adjusts the score based on the long-term significance of the deals. This helps account for qualitative factors such as entering new markets or securing high-value, strategic customers.

This formula combines profitability, efficiency, and strategic impact into a single metric to provide a holistic view of sales team performance. Let's take a look at how it applies to three different scenarios:

Scenario 1: Technology Sales Team

- **Total Sales:** 15

- **Average Deal Size:** $100,000

- **Margin:** 30% (or $30,000 per deal)

- **Customer Acquisition Cost (CAC):** $10,000

- **Conversion Rate:** 20%

- **Strategic Importance Weight:** 0.9 (The team is focused on acquiring clients in a key market.)

SSI Calculation:

$$SSI = \frac{(15 \times 100{,}000 \times 0.30)}{10{,}000} \times 0.20 \times 0.9$$

1. **Total Sales x Avg. Deal Size x Margin** = 15 × $100,000 × 0.30 = $450,000
2. **Divide by CAC** = $450,000 ÷ $10,000 = 45
3. **Multiply by Conversion Rate** = 45 × 0.20 = 9
4. **Multiply by Strategic Importance Weight** = 9 × 0.9 = **8.1**

SSI Score: **8.1**

Interpretation: This tech sales team is performing well, acquiring clients in a strategically important market with large deal sizes and healthy margins.

Scenario 2: Retail Sales Team

- **Total Sales:** 50
- **Average Deal Size:** $2,000
- **Margin:** 15% (or $300 per deal)
- **Customer Acquisition Cost (CAC):** $250
- **Conversion Rate:** 10%
- **Strategic Importance Weight:** 0.7 (Focus on everyday products with modest strategic value.)

SSI Calculation:

$$SSI = \frac{(50 \times 2{,}000 \times 0.15)}{250} \times 0.10 \times 0.7$$

1. **Total Sales x Avg. Deal Size x Margin** = 50 × $2,000 × 0.15 = $15,000
2. **Divide by CAC** = $15,000 ÷ $250 = 60
3. **Multiply by Conversion Rate** = 60 × 0.10 = 6
4. **Multiply by Strategic Importance Weight** = 6 × 0.7 = **4.2**

SSI Score: **4.2**

Interpretation: This retail sales team is doing a decent job, but improving conversion rates and focusing on more strategically valuable deals would help boost their SSI.

Scenario 3: Healthcare Sales Team

- **Total Sales:** 8
- **Average Deal Size:** $75,000
- **Margin:** 40% (or $30,000 per deal)
- **Customer Acquisition Cost (CAC):** $15,000
- **Conversion Rate:** 30%
- **Strategic Importance Weight:** 1.0 (These sales are critical for entering a high-growth healthcare market.)

SSI Calculation:

$$SSI = \frac{(8 \times 75{,}000 \times 0.40)}{15{,}000} \times 0.30 \times 1.0$$

1. **Total Sales x Avg. Deal Size x Margin** = 8 × $75,000 × 0.40 = $240,000
2. **Divide by CAC** = $240,000 ÷ $15,000 = 16
3. **Multiply by Conversion Rate** = 16 × 0.30 = 4.8
4. **Multiply by Strategic Importance Weight** = 4.8 × 1.0 = **4.8**

SSI Score: **4.8**

Interpretation: The healthcare team is working with highly strategic deals in a growing market, but improving their conversion rate could help increase their overall SSI score

In each scenario, the **Sales Success Index (SSI)** provides a clear and quantifiable measure of how well the sales teams are performing, considering not just raw sales numbers but also efficiency, profitability, and strategic value. This makes the SSI a versatile and valuable tool for sales teams across various industries and product or service-based markets.

Example of KPI Integration

For businesses, understanding the relationship between KPIs like Customer Acquisition Cost (CAC) and conversion rates can help optimize both marketing and sales strategies. For example, a company that notices a high CAC but a low conversion rate may need to focus on improving lead quality or refining its sales messaging. Conversely, if conversion rates are high but CAC is also rising, it may be worth exploring cost-saving measures in the marketing funnel to improve profitability[42].

By tracking these KPIs consistently and using tools like Tableau to visualize them, sales leaders can make informed, strategic decisions that drive growth, improve team performance, and ensure that resources are allocated effectively. KPIs provide a roadmap for continuous improvement, guiding sales teams to focus on the areas that have the most significant impact on success.

Conducting Effective Sales Performance Reviews

Performance reviews are a cornerstone of success in any sales organization, serving as a key tool for assessing both individual and team effectiveness. For small businesses, where resources may be limited, sales leaders must take a strategic approach to these reviews, leveraging data to ensure that they are meaningful and actionable. When done correctly, performance reviews not only enhance employee performance but also ensure that individual efforts align with broader organizational objectives. By creating a structured, data-driven review process, sales teams can foster a culture of continuous improvement and maintain focus on their goals.

1. Set Clear Expectations

Before conducting a performance review, it is crucial to ensure that all sales team members understand the metrics and goals by which they will be evaluated. This clarity creates a fair and transparent review process, reducing the potential for misunderstandings and ensuring that everyone is aligned on expectations.

- **Communicate Metrics:** The foundation of any effective performance review is clear communication. Sales leaders should

[42] https://www.netsuite.com/portal/resource/articles/accounting/sales-kpis.shtml

outline the Key Performance Indicators (KPIs) that will be used to measure success. Common KPIs in sales include conversion rates, average deal size, and customer acquisition costs. By clearly communicating these metrics early on, employees will know exactly what is expected of them and can focus their efforts accordingly. For example, a sales rep who knows that conversion rate is a key metric can prioritize nurturing high-quality leads to improve this figure[43].

- **Establish a Rubric:** Creating a standardized performance review template that includes specific criteria for each role within the sales team is essential. This rubric should be shared with employees during onboarding, setting clear expectations from the outset. The rubric might cover key areas such as lead generation, customer engagement, closing techniques, and time management. When employees understand how they will be evaluated, they can better align their actions with the company's expectations, leading to more consistent performance.

2. Use Data to Drive Insights

Data-driven insights are crucial for guiding performance reviews, ensuring that evaluations are objective and focused on measurable outcomes. By reviewing KPIs like conversion rates, average deal size, and sales cycle length, sales leaders can gain a comprehensive view of both individual and team performance.

- **Analyze Performance Metrics:** Leveraging tools like CRM systems allow sales leaders to track and analyze individual and team performance. For instance, tracking metrics like the average time to convert a lead or the number of contracts signed

---

[43] https://onstrategyhq.com/resources/27-examples-of-key-performance-indicators/

in a quarter provides valuable insights into the effectiveness of sales strategies. These data points highlight specific strengths and areas for improvement. If a salesperson is consistently exceeding their average deal size target but falling short of conversion rates, this might suggest that while they're skilled at closing high-value deals, they may need support in prospecting or lead nurturing.

- **Identify Trends:** Beyond analyzing individual metrics, it's essential to look for trends in the data that can indicate broader strengths or weaknesses in the sales process. For example, if conversion rates are consistently declining across the team, this could point to a systemic issue that needs to be addressed, whether that's through additional training, adjustments to the sales pitch, or refining the target audience. Identifying these trends early allows sales leaders to take proactive measures to course-correct before the issues negatively impact the bottom line[44].

3. Provide Constructive Feedback

Feedback is one of the most powerful tools for fostering a culture of continuous improvement within the sales team. However, the way feedback is delivered can make all the difference in its effectiveness. Sales leaders should aim to offer constructive, actionable feedback that motivates employees to grow and improve.

- **Be Specific:** Vague feedback like "you need to improve your numbers" does little to guide employees on how they can perform better. Instead, provide concrete examples of both successes and opportunities for growth during the review. For instance, rather than saying, "You need to improve your follow-

---

[44]https://keap.com/small-business-automation-blog/sales/sales-process/sales-performance-reviews-5-best-practices-to-optimize-performance

up," a more actionable piece of feedback might be, "I've noticed that many of your leads go cold after the initial contact. Let's work on developing a more structured follow-up process to keep prospects engaged[45]."

- **Encourage Development:** Feedback should not only point out areas for improvement but also offer a pathway for development—frame feedback in a way that encourages team members to focus on professional growth. For example, if an employee is struggling with closing high-value deals, you might suggest a specific sales training program that could help them refine their negotiation skills. This approach not only addresses performance issues but also empowers employees to take ownership of their development[46].

4. Set SMART Goals

As part of the performance review process, it's important to collaborate with your sales team to set SMART (Specific, Measurable, Achievable, Relevant, Time-bound) goals. These goals provide a clear roadmap for success and align individual performance with broader company objectives.

- **Define SMART Goals:** Vague goals like "improve sales" do little to motivate or guide employees. Instead, SMART goals provide clear, actionable targets. For example, rather than saying, "Increase sales," a SMART goal would be: "Increase monthly sales by 20% over the next quarter by targeting new customer segments and leveraging referral programs." This level of specificity not only makes the goal more achievable but

---

45 https://www.kennect.io/post/sales-performance-evaluation

46 https://wystra.com/performance-review-in-small-companies-best-practices

also ensures that both the sales leader and the employee have a clear understanding of what success looks like.

- **Track Progress:** Setting goals is only half the battle—regularly tracking progress toward these goals is just as important. Sales leaders should monitor key metrics throughout the year to ensure that employees are staying on track. This ongoing evaluation helps maintain accountability and allows for adjustments as needed based on performance trends. For example, if a sales rep is on pace to exceed their quarterly goal, the leader might encourage them to push for a stretch goal or explore additional opportunities for upselling or cross-selling.

Implementing Feedback Loops for Ongoing Improvement

Continuous improvement in sales processes and customer satisfaction is essential for long-term success in any business. Feedback loops provide a structured and systematic way to gather insights from both customers and internal teams, allowing sales leaders to make data-driven adjustments that enhance performance and efficiency. By actively implementing feedback mechanisms, organizations can stay responsive to changing needs and continuously optimize their strategies. Feedback loops ensure that sales teams not only address immediate issues but also build a foundation for sustained success and innovation.

1. Customer Feedback

Gathering customer feedback is vital for understanding satisfaction levels, preferences, and pain points. Customers are the ultimate judges of a company's products and services, and their feedback provides a direct path to refining sales approaches, enhancing product offerings, and improving customer experiences. Implementing effective channels to gather customer insights ensures that businesses remain attuned to the evolving needs of their clientele.

- **Surveys:** One of the most efficient methods for collecting customer feedback is through surveys. Surveys can be distributed via email, integrated into websites, or conducted in person, and they offer flexibility in format. Common survey tools include Net Promoter Score (NPS) to measure customer loyalty, Customer Satisfaction Score (CSAT) to gauge customer happiness, and open-ended questions for deeper insights. For instance, an NPS survey might ask customers how likely they are to recommend the company's product to others, while open-ended questions allow customers to explain why they may have hesitations or what they loved about their experience.

- **Interviews:** Conducting one-on-one interviews with customers provides deeper, qualitative insights into their experiences and expectations. While surveys are great for gathering broad data, interviews allow for more detailed conversations, revealing nuances that surveys might miss. These direct interactions help uncover specific pain points or desires that can guide product development or sales tactics. For example, during an interview, a customer might share that while they love the product's features, the onboarding process felt confusing, highlighting an opportunity to improve the user experience.

- **Social Media Monitoring:** In today's digital age, social media platforms are a goldmine for real-time customer feedback. Actively monitoring platforms like Twitter, Instagram, LinkedIn, and Facebook for mentions of your brand provides immediate insight into customer sentiment. Engaging with customers directly on social media not only helps gather feedback but also fosters a sense of community and responsiveness. For instance, if a customer praises your product on social media, you can acknowledge their feedback publicly, strengthening the brand-customer relationship.

- **In-App Feedback:** For businesses with mobile or web applications, integrating in-app feedback tools allows users to provide comments and ratings directly within the app. This method captures user experiences in real-time, making it easier to identify usability issues, bugs, or desired features. By collecting feedback while the experience is fresh in the user's mind, businesses can address issues faster and more efficiently. For example, a user struggling with a new app feature may leave a comment about its functionality, giving the company an opportunity to improve the feature based on real user experience[47].

By systematically collecting and analyzing customer feedback, sales leaders can identify trends and areas needing improvement. This continuous feedback loop ensures that products and services evolve in alignment with customer expectations, ultimately leading to better customer satisfaction and loyalty.

2. Internal Team Feedback

Sales representatives are often the first point of contact with customers, making them a critical source of insight into what works well and what does not in the sales process. Encouraging open communication within the sales team fosters a culture of collaboration, transparency, and continuous improvement. By actively seeking internal feedback, sales leaders can identify areas for training, coaching, and optimization while also empowering their teams to contribute to process improvements.

- **Regular Check-ins:** Establishing regular one-on-one meetings between sales managers and team members is essential for ongoing dialogue about performance, challenges, and successes. These check-ins provide an opportunity for sales reps to share their on-the-ground experiences while managers can offer support and guidance. By focusing on both qualitative feedback (personal experiences) and quantitative metrics (sales performance data), these meetings ensure that feedback is balanced and constructive. For example, a sales rep might highlight that they are consistently facing pushback on pricing,

---

47 https://www.surveysensum.com/blog/collect-customer-feedback

prompting the manager to consider pricing flexibility or additional sales training.

- **360-Degree Feedback:** Implementing a 360-degree feedback system allows employees to receive input from peers, subordinates, and supervisors, providing a holistic view of their performance. This method not only evaluates how effectively a salesperson interacts with customers but also assesses how they collaborate with other team members. The well-rounded nature of 360-degree feedback can reveal hidden strengths and areas for development that might otherwise go unnoticed, ensuring that performance reviews are more comprehensive and fair.

- **Feedback Forums:** Creating dedicated channels or forums where team members can share insights or suggestions promotes a culture of collaboration and continuous improvement. These forums can be physical (like weekly team meetings) or digital (such as a Slack channel or intranet forum). Allowing team members to share their ideas or concerns in an open forum, whether publicly or anonymously, creates a sense of shared responsibility for the success of the sales team. For instance, a sales rep might suggest a more efficient lead qualification process based on their experience, which could lead to a process improvement benefiting the entire team[48].

- **Recognition Programs:** Acknowledging contributions from team members is crucial for maintaining morale and fostering a positive work environment. Recognition programs, whether formal (like Employee of the Month awards) or informal (like shout-outs during team meetings), can motivate team members to continue sharing valuable insights. Celebrating success

---

[48]https://www.launchnotes.com/blog/the-ultimate-guide-to-internal-feedback-in-the-workplace

publicly reinforces the value of feedback within the organization, as employees see that their contributions are recognized and appreciated. This, in turn, encourages more open communication and innovation within the team[49].

By actively seeking internal feedback and integrating it into performance reviews and strategy sessions, sales leaders can foster a culture of continuous improvement. This proactive approach not only improves team dynamics but also enhances processes and drives overall sales performance. When sales reps feel heard and valued, they are more motivated to contribute to the team's success, leading to better outcomes for both the organization and its customers.

In summary, measuring sales success and driving continuous improvement are at the heart of any thriving sales organization. By integrating data-driven tools, tracking key performance indicators, and fostering a culture of continuous feedback and process refinement, businesses can ensure their sales strategies remain agile and effective. It's not just about hitting sales targets but about creating a sustainable system where every action is informed by clear insights and the potential for growth is constantly being unlocked.

In today's competitive environment, those who embrace continuous improvement using data visualization tools, Six Sigma methodologies, and structured performance reviews are better positioned to adapt to market changes and customer needs. By measuring success holistically and refining processes through feedback loops, sales teams can evolve with confidence, driving both immediate results and long-term gains. The key is persistence, adaptability, and a relentless focus on excellence.

---

[49] https://www.180ops.com/180-perspective-change/role-of-feedback-in-enhancing-sales-performance

CHAPTER 7

Staying Ahead of the Competition

"To be successful, you have to have your heart in your business, and your business in your heart."

— **Thomas Watson Sr.**

In today's hyper-competitive world of business sales, staying ahead of the competition is not just a goal; it's a necessity. As markets evolve and competitor strategies become more sophisticated, businesses must sharpen their understanding of market dynamics and be ready to adapt at a moment's notice. Success demands a combination of strategic insight and agility, allowing you to respond quickly to shifting landscapes while maintaining a forward-thinking vision.

This chapter will explore key tools such as Porter's Five Forces, a competitive analysis framework that will help you dissect market competition and identify the factors influencing your industry. We'll also dive into agile methodologies, offering businesses the flexibility to respond to rapid changes in market conditions. Through practical examples, tools, and strategies, you'll discover how to position your business for sustainable, long-term success. Whether you're tracking competitors or navigating unpredictable market shifts, mastering these concepts will give you the edge you need to stay ahead of the pack.

Porter's Five Forces- Understanding Market Dynamics

Porter's Five Forces framework is an essential tool for sales leaders looking to navigate the complex, competitive landscape of their industry. This strategic framework helps leaders understand the various forces that shape the market, anticipate challenges, and make informed decisions to strengthen their position. By analyzing these forces, businesses can develop strategies to mitigate risks and capitalize on opportunities, ensuring they stay competitive in a rapidly evolving marketplace. Let's delve into each of the five forces and explore how businesses can apply them to gain a competitive edge.

1. Threat of New Entrants

The threat of new entrants assesses how easily new competitors can enter the market and disrupt existing players. For existing businesses, the ease with which newcomers can compete depends on factors like barriers to entry, which may include:

- **Specialized Knowledge:** If your industry requires specialized expertise or technical skills, new entrants may struggle to match the quality of your products or services. This gives established businesses an advantage.

- **Significant Startup Costs:** Industries with high startup costs, such as expensive technology, infrastructure, or equipment, tend to discourage potential new competitors. Businesses can use these high initial costs to their advantage by continually investing in cutting-edge technology or infrastructure, ensuring that newcomers face higher financial hurdles.

- **Brand Loyalty:** A strong, loyal customer base can act as a significant barrier to entry. If customers are deeply attached to your brand, new entrants may find it difficult to convince them to switch. For existing businesses, building strong relationships with customers and cultivating brand loyalty through personalized service or community engagement can act as a shield against new competitors.

Strategy Tip: Firms can fortify their market position by creating a strong brand identity, investing in customer loyalty programs, and continuously improving customer relationships. These strategies not only make it harder for new competitors to enter the market but also solidify your standing in the minds of your customers[50].

2. Bargaining Power of Suppliers

The bargaining power of suppliers refers to the influence that suppliers can exert on a business, particularly regarding pricing, terms of supply, and availability of key materials. If a business relies heavily on a few suppliers, those suppliers may have considerable leverage, affecting profitability and flexibility. For small businesses, this dynamic can be particularly challenging, as they may lack the purchasing power of larger companies.

- **Supplier Dependency:** A limited supplier pool can lead to higher costs or supply disruptions, especially if those suppliers dominate the market or have few competitors.

- **Diversification of Suppliers:** To mitigate this risk, small businesses should consider diversifying their supplier base or negotiating favorable long-term contracts to reduce dependency on any single supplier. Having multiple suppliers not only provides flexibility but also enhances your ability to negotiate better pricing and terms.

Strategy Tip: Sales leaders can protect their margins by building strong relationships with a range of suppliers and exploring alternative sources. This diversification strategy ensures that businesses are less vulnerable to price hikes or supply chain disruptions, ultimately preserving profitability[51].

---

[50]https://copymate.app/blog/multi/porters-five-forces-analysis-understanding-the-dynamics-of-competition-in-your-industry/

[51] https://www.forbes.com/advisor/business/porters-five-forces/

3. Bargaining Power of Buyers

The bargaining power of buyers refers to the influence that customers can have over pricing, product quality, and service offerings. In markets where customers have multiple alternatives and low switching costs, they can exert pressure on businesses to lower prices, offer more features, or improve service quality. This can squeeze margins, particularly for small businesses.

- **Buyer Influence:** If customers can easily switch between competitors, they may use their purchasing power to demand lower prices or better terms, which can erode profitability. For instance, in highly competitive industries like retail or technology, where products are similar, buyers have significant leverage.
- **Building Loyalty:** To counter this, small businesses should focus on delivering unique value propositions that set them apart from competitors. Offering personalized customer service, exclusive products, or loyalty programs can make switching less attractive for buyers, reducing their bargaining power.

Strategy Tip: To diminish buyer power, businesses should concentrate on strengthening customer relationships and enhancing brand loyalty. Implementing loyalty programs, providing exceptional customer service, or offering customized solutions can create a more compelling reason for customers to stay, reducing their likelihood of switching to competitors.

4. Threat of Substitute Products or Services

The threat of substitutes considers the risk of customers switching to alternative products or services that fulfill the same need. These substitutes may come from direct competitors, or they could emerge from new technologies or innovations that render existing offerings obsolete. In an era of rapid technological advancement, this threat is especially relevant for small businesses.

- **Technological Innovation:** The rise of new technologies can create substitutes that directly threaten existing products. For example, digital streaming services have replaced traditional DVDs, and ride-sharing apps have disrupted the taxi industry. Small businesses need to stay vigilant, keeping a close eye on emerging trends and technological advancements that could reshape their industry.

- **Continuous Innovation:** To safeguard against the threat of substitutes, businesses should continuously innovate and adapt their offerings. By staying ahead of market trends and anticipating customer needs, small businesses can ensure that their products or services remain relevant, even in the face of new competition.

Strategy Tip: Regularly invest in market research and innovation to stay ahead of potential substitutes. Understanding customer needs and evolving market conditions allows businesses to adapt quickly, ensuring their offerings remain competitive and relevant in a changing landscape[52].

5. Industry Rivalry

Industry rivalry refers to the intensity of competition among existing businesses in the same industry. High levels of rivalry often lead to price wars, aggressive marketing strategies, and a constant need for innovation. For businesses, understanding the competitive landscape is crucial for standing out and securing their share of the market.

- **Price Competition:** In industries with an intense rivalry, businesses may resort to lowering prices to gain market share. However, this can lead to shrinking profit margins. Businesses

[52] https://www.investopedia.com/terms/p/porter.asp

must be cautious about engaging in price wars, as they often lack the financial reserves of larger competitors.

- **Differentiation:** Instead of competing solely on price, businesses should focus on differentiation—whether through product quality, superior customer service, or niche offerings. By highlighting unique aspects of their brand, they can create a competitive advantage that allows them to thrive even in a crowded market.

Strategy Tip: Businesses can excel by differentiating their offerings, targeting niche markets, or providing exceptional customer experiences. Focusing on these areas helps create a competitive edge and minimizes the risk of being drawn into costly price wars[53].

Analyzing and Monitoring Competitors

In the ever-evolving world of sales, understanding your competition is critical for staying ahead. For sales leaders, continuous analysis and monitoring of competitors is not just a reactive strategy—it's a proactive approach to uncover opportunities for differentiation and mitigate market threats. By tracking competitor actions, identifying strengths and weaknesses, and strategically positioning your offerings, you can gain the upper hand in an increasingly competitive marketplace. Here's a detailed guide to help business leaders effectively analyze and monitor their competitors.

---

[53]https://www.linkedin.com/pulse/how-porters-five-forces-helps-small-businesses-music-group-llc

1. Identify Competitors

The first step in a competitor analysis is building a comprehensive list of both direct and indirect competitors. This foundational step sets the stage for deeper analysis, allowing you to understand your competitive landscape fully.

- **Direct Competitors:** These are businesses that offer the same or similar products and services to the same target audience as your own. For example, if you run a local coffee shop, other nearby coffee shops that attract the same customers are your direct competitors. Direct competitors vie for the same market share, and understanding their strategies helps you position your offerings more effectively.

- **Indirect Competitors:** Indirect competitors provide different solutions to similar problems or cater to a related market. For example, your coffee shop might face indirect competition from nearby juice bars or tea houses that offer alternative beverages to the same health-conscious customer base. While they don't compete head-to-head with your product, they still draw customers away from your business.

Identifying both direct and indirect competitors allows you to build a complete picture of the competitive landscape. Tools like Google, industry-specific directories, and social media platforms can help you conduct thorough research and ensure that you're aware of all potential competitors, both obvious and less apparent[54].

---

[54] https://asana.com/resources/competitive-analysis-example

2. Monitor Competitor Actions

Monitoring competitors is essential for staying ahead in the game. By keeping an eye on their actions, you can anticipate their next move and adjust your strategy accordingly. Here's how to track key areas:

- **Marketing Campaigns:** Pay close attention to how competitors position themselves in the market through advertising, promotions, and social media engagement. Tools like SEMrush, Ahrefs, and Google Alerts allow you to track their SEO performance, keyword strategies, and content marketing tactics. Analyzing their messaging can reveal how they're attracting customers and provide insights into where you can differentiate.

- **Product Launches:** Keeping track of new product releases and feature rollouts can help you anticipate shifts in customer preferences and industry trends. Competitor product launches often signal where the market is heading, allowing you to pivot or enhance your own offerings before falling behind. For example, if a competitor launches a product with a feature your offering lacks, you might consider prioritizing a similar feature in your product roadmap or, alternatively, emphasizing other unique benefits of your offering.

- **Pricing Strategies:** Regularly reviewing competitor pricing models is critical for ensuring that your products or services remain competitively priced. This includes analyzing how competitors use discounts, bundles, or subscription models to attract customers. Are they lowering prices, offering special promotions, or introducing value-added services? By understanding their pricing tactics, you can strategically position your own offerings to appeal to cost-conscious consumers or highlight the superior value of your product.

- **Customer Engagement:** Monitoring how competitors interact with their customers on social media platforms, forums, and review sites provides valuable insights into their strengths and weaknesses. Do they respond quickly to customer queries or complaints? Are customers satisfied with their interactions? Engaging with this information helps you identify gaps in their customer service that you can exploit by offering a superior customer experience[55].

To streamline the process of monitoring competitors, tools like Google Alerts, Mention, and Hootsuite can automate tracking and send you notifications when significant changes occur in your competitors' strategies.

3. Evaluate Strengths and Weaknesses

A comprehensive evaluation of your competitors' strengths and weaknesses is the key to identifying areas where your business can outperform them. This step involves conducting a detailed assessment to uncover opportunities for differentiation.

- **SWOT Analysis (Strengths, Weaknesses, Opportunities, Threats):** Conducting a SWOT analysis for each major competitor allows you to take a structured approach to competitor evaluation. This analysis will help you understand what your competitors do well—such as having strong brand recognition or an efficient supply chain—and where they fall short—such as poor customer service or a limited product range. For instance, if a competitor is known for innovative product features but lacks customer service, you can capitalize on this weakness by emphasizing your exceptional customer support in marketing materials.

- **Benchmarking:** Comparing your key performance indicators (KPIs) against those of your competitors is another essential

[55]https://asymmetric.pro/understanding-competitor-analysis-a-comprehensive-guide-for-business-leaders/

method for identifying competitive advantages or areas for improvement. Metrics like customer satisfaction scores, market share, sales revenue, and conversion rates provide valuable data points that can highlight where your business excels or where it lags. For example, if your competitor has a higher customer retention rate, it may signal that you need to invest more in relationship-building initiatives such as loyalty programs or follow-up communication[56].

Strategy Tip: Identifying both strengths and weaknesses not only helps you understand where you stand in relation to your competitors but also allows you to focus your efforts on areas that can deliver the greatest competitive advantage. By zeroing in on gaps in the market, you can tailor your offerings to meet unfulfilled customer needs or offer superior alternatives.

Example- Pivoting Strategy Based on Competitor Analysis

Consider the case of a software development firm offering project management tools. During a routine competitive analysis, they noticed that a key competitor had launched an aggressive marketing campaign centered around a new feature that their product lacked. Instead of scrambling to match the feature, the firm chose to conduct a thorough competitor analysis to assess strengths and weaknesses.

Through their analysis, they discovered that while the competitor's new feature was indeed attractive, customer reviews frequently cited dissatisfaction with their customer support. The firm decided to pivot by doubling down on its personalized customer service, an area where it already excelled. By improving their customer support systems and marketing these improvements, they were able to carve out a niche in the market, emphasizing that while their competitor might

---

[56] https://venngage.com/blog/competitor-analysis-template/

offer more features, they delivered a superior user experience through dedicated support.

This strategic pivot allowed them to differentiate without engaging in a costly "feature race." Instead, they created a strong brand position centered around customer care—an often overlooked but critical factor in long-term customer loyalty.

Developing Unique Selling Propositions (USPs) for Business Sales Leaders

In today's competitive marketplace, businesses need to stand out in order to thrive. A well-defined Unique Selling Proposition (USP) is the cornerstone of any effective differentiation strategy. It clearly communicates what sets your business apart from the competition and why customers should choose your product or service. For sales leaders, crafting a compelling USP not only attracts customers but fosters brand loyalty and drives long-term revenue growth. Here's a structured approach to developing a USP that resonates with your audience and creates a competitive edge.

1. Understand Your Target Market

The foundation of any compelling USP is a deep understanding of your target market. To resonate with your audience, you must first know who they are, what they care about, and what challenges they face.

- **Identify Customer Pain Points:** Start by researching the specific problems or needs your customers have. This can be done through surveys, focus groups, or one-on-one interviews. Understanding these pain points allows you to tailor your product or service to the ideal solution. For example, if you're selling eco-friendly products, your customers might be looking for sustainable alternatives to everyday items. By addressing this need, you position your product as the go-to solution for environmentally conscious consumers.

- **Define Your Audience:** Market segmentation is key to ensuring your USP resonates with the right audience. Divide your target market based on demographics, psychographics, and buying behavior. Are you targeting health-conscious millennials, busy professionals looking for convenience, or families seeking affordable solutions? For example, a local bakery might target health-conscious consumers who value organic, locally sourced ingredients. The more precisely you define your audience, the more impactful your USP will be.

By aligning your product or service with the needs and desires of your target audience, you create a USP that speaks directly to them, making your offerings more attractive and relevant.

2. Analyze Competitors

The next step in developing a USP is understanding the competitive landscape. A thorough analysis of your competitors will reveal gaps in the market and opportunities for differentiation.

- **Evaluate Competitor Offerings:** Take a close look at the products or services your competitors offer. What are their strengths and weaknesses? Use competitor analysis tools like SEMrush, SimilarWeb, or customer reviews to gather insights. Are they known for low prices but lack in customer service? Do they offer a wide variety of products but struggle with delivery times?

- **Identify Market Gaps:** Once you have a clear understanding of what competitors are doing, look for areas where they fall short. These gaps present opportunities for your business to stand out. For example, if your competitors offer similar products but lack personalized customer service, you can focus on providing a more hands-on, tailored experience. Similarly, if competitors are slow to innovate, your business could capitalize by offering cutting-edge solutions that better meet customer needs.

Strategy Tip: By identifying where competitors fail to meet customer expectations, you can position your USP to fill those gaps, ensuring your offerings provide a solution that customers can't find elsewhere.

3. Highlight Your Strengths

Once you've identified your target market and analyzed your competitors, the next step is to focus on what makes your business truly unique. Your USP should highlight the strengths that differentiate your business from the rest.

- **Core Competencies:** Identify the specific strengths that your business brings to the table. Whether it's exceptional customer service, innovative product features, or a commitment to sustainability, your USP should reflect the core competencies that set you apart. For example, a software company might emphasize its intuitive user interface and dedicated customer support team as key differentiators in a crowded market.
- **Value Proposition:** Clearly articulate the unique benefits that your product or service provides. What makes your offering better, faster, or more convenient than the competition? A well-defined value proposition not only sets you apart but can also justify premium pricing. For instance, a business selling luxury skincare products might emphasize the use of rare, organic ingredients sourced from sustainable farms. By focusing on these unique features, they can justify higher prices while appealing to eco-conscious consumers.

Strategy Tip: Highlighting your strengths and communicating the added value of your offerings not only differentiates your business but also enables you to build brand loyalty and potentially command higher prices[57].

4. Integrate Your USP Everywhere

Your USP is not just a tagline—it's the essence of what makes your business unique. Once you've developed your USP, it's essential to integrate it across every touchpoint of your business to ensure consistency and brand recognition.

- **Marketing Materials:** Your USP should be prominently featured in all marketing collateral, including brochures, websites, social media profiles, email campaigns, and advertisements. By consistently showcasing your USP, you reinforce the message that sets your business apart, ensuring that it sticks in the minds of your target audience. For instance, if your USP focuses on sustainability, make sure this message is woven into your website content, social media posts, and product packaging.

- **Sales Interactions:** Train your sales team to communicate your USP effectively during customer interactions. Whether through phone calls, face-to-face meetings, or online chats, salespeople should consistently reference the unique benefits your business offers. This ensures that your brand identity is reinforced at every stage of the customer journey, building trust and making it easier to close deals.

- **Customer Experience:** Your USP should not only be part of your marketing message but should also be reflected in the customer experience. For example, if your USP highlights

---

[57]https://inventora.com/why-your-small-business-needs-a-unique-selling-proposition/

"handcrafted, organic pastries made from locally sourced ingredients," ensure that every product your bakery sells lives up to this promise—from sourcing to presentation. This consistency between your USP and the actual customer experience helps build credibility and strengthens customer loyalty.

Strategy Tip: Consistent messaging across all customer touchpoints helps solidify your brand identity and ensures that your USP becomes synonymous with your business. This level of consistency builds trust and fosters customer loyalty, encouraging repeat business[58] [59].

Example of a Compelling USP

Let's consider the case of a local bakery. Their USP could be: "Handcrafted, organic pastries made from locally sourced ingredients." This USP appeals to consumers who prioritize quality, sustainability, and supporting local businesses. By focusing on values such as organic sourcing and artisanal craftsmanship, the bakery distinguishes itself from larger chains that may emphasize convenience or lower prices but lack the same personal touch or ethical considerations.

This USP resonates with health-conscious consumers and those who want to make environmentally responsible choices. By marketing this USP consistently across all platforms—social media, in-store displays, and customer interactions—the bakery not only attracts its ideal customer base but also builds a loyal community that values its core principles.

---

[58] https://www.optimizely.com/optimization-glossary/unique-selling-point/

[59] https://www.entrepreneur.com/encyclopedia/unique-selling-proposition-usp

Adapting to Market Changes and Trends

In today's fast-paced and ever-evolving sales environment, business leaders must continuously adapt to rapidly changing market conditions. These changes can stem from technological advancements, shifts in consumer preferences, and external economic factors. For businesses, agility and responsiveness are not just desirable—they're essential for both survival and growth. Below are key strategies that sales leaders can implement to ensure their businesses remain adaptable in a constantly changing landscape.

1. Stay Informed

Staying informed is the foundation of adaptability. In a competitive and dynamic market, businesses need to anticipate trends, be aware of emerging technologies, and monitor competitor activities to stay one step ahead. Sales leaders who proactively gather information can make strategic adjustments before shifts in the market affect their bottom line.

- **Industry Reports:** Subscribing to industry-specific reports and market research platforms such as IBISWorld, Statista, or Gartner offers critical insights into market dynamics, customer behaviors, and emerging trends. These resources provide a wealth of data on industry growth projections, competitive landscapes, and consumer demands, allowing sales leaders to stay ahead of the curve. For example, a retail business might notice a growing trend toward eco-friendly products in industry reports and use that insight to shift product offerings before competitors catch on.

- **Trade Shows and Conferences:** Attending trade shows and industry conferences gives business leaders firsthand exposure to new technologies, competitor innovations, and consumer trends. These events offer opportunities to network with industry peers, form partnerships, and gather ideas for enhancing business offerings. Whether it's discovering new sales tools or witnessing cutting-edge technologies, these experiences help sales leaders remain connected to the pulse of their industry.

- **Social Listening:** Engaging in social listening through tools like Hootsuite or Brandwatch allows businesses to monitor customer sentiment, market trends, and competitor activities in real-time. By analyzing social media conversations and online reviews, sales leaders can detect emerging trends, respond to customer concerns quickly, and capitalize on new opportunities. For example, a company noticing rising demand for a specific feature in social conversations can adjust its product strategy to meet this demand.

By continuously monitoring the industry, sales leaders are better positioned to make informed, data-driven decisions that align with market shifts. Proactive knowledge gathering ensures that businesses are not blindsided by change but instead embrace it as an opportunity to innovate.

2. Be Open to Innovation

Innovation is the lifeblood of business adaptability. As new technologies and methodologies emerge, businesses that are willing to embrace change will have a significant competitive advantage. Innovation allows businesses to enhance customer experiences, streamline operations, and stay ahead of competitors.

- **Embrace New Technologies:** Technology is constantly evolving, and businesses must be open to integrating new tools into their sales strategies. For instance, adopting Customer Relationship Management (CRM) systems like HubSpot or Salesforce can revolutionize how a business manages customer interactions, tracks leads and improves communication. In a data-driven world, CRMs help sales teams gather valuable insights about customer behaviors, preferences, and buying patterns, enabling them to personalize their approach and close more deals.

- **Agile Methodologies:** Implementing agile methodologies, such as SCRUM, empowers sales teams to remain flexible and responsive in their strategies. The iterative nature of agile processes encourages teams to test new ideas, gather feedback, and make quick adjustments. This approach fosters a culture of experimentation and continuous improvement, enabling businesses to adapt to changing market conditions with greater ease. For example, an e-commerce business using agile practices may run a short-term promotional campaign and tweak its messaging based on real-time customer feedback.

Being open to innovation enables businesses to keep up with industry advancements and create a more efficient, customer-focused sales approach. Businesses that resist innovation risk becoming outdated and losing market share to more agile competitors.

3. Gather Customer Feedback

Customer feedback is a goldmine of information when it comes to adapting to market changes. Understanding customer needs, preferences, and pain points allows businesses to pivot quickly and fine-tune their offerings to meet evolving demands better.

- **Surveys and Direct Conversations:** Regularly conducting surveys or engaging in direct conversations with customers provides invaluable insights into their preferences and experiences. Tools like SurveyMonkey and Typeform make it easy to gather this feedback, while in-person or phone interviews can offer deeper insights into customer satisfaction and unmet needs. By maintaining an open line of communication with customers, sales leaders can identify areas for improvement and develop strategies that directly address customer expectations.

- **Customer Reviews:** Monitoring online reviews on platforms such as Google My Business, Yelp, and Trustpilot offers a window into the customer experience. These reviews reveal both the strengths and weaknesses of your offerings. Addressing issues raised in reviews demonstrates to customers that their feedback is valued, leading to improved loyalty and satisfaction. For example, a restaurant that consistently receives feedback about slow service can implement operational changes to reduce wait times and enhance the dining experience.

By actively gathering and analyzing customer feedback, businesses can stay attuned to shifts in customer preferences and expectations, ensuring they remain competitive in a changing marketplace.

Example- Adapting to Changing Market Conditions

A prime example of adaptability can be seen in a business that specializes in printed marketing materials. Initially, the company experienced significant growth by providing traditional print services like brochures, business cards, and posters. However, as digital media began to dominate, the business noticed a sharp decline in demand for printed materials.

Rather than clinging to outdated methods, the business made a strategic pivot. After conducting market research and gathering customer feedback, they decided to expand their services to include digital marketing solutions, such as web design, social media management, and online branding. By diversifying its service offerings, the company was able to retain its existing customer base while attracting a new segment of clients focused on digital solutions.

This shift not only saved the business from the decline in print media but also opened the door to new revenue streams. The business leveraged its expertise in branding and design to transition seamlessly into the digital marketing space, proving that adaptability is the key to survival—and growth—in a rapidly changing market.

Bringing this chapter to a close, staying ahead of the competition requires more than just reacting to market shifts; it demands a proactive approach rooted in deep market analysis, continuous innovation, and a keen understanding of both customer and competitor dynamics. Sales leaders who effectively analyze their competitive landscape, develop unique selling propositions, and adapt quickly to changing trends will not only survive but thrive in an increasingly competitive marketplace.

By leveraging tools like Porter's Five Forces, monitoring competitors, and building a compelling USP, businesses can carve out a distinct market position. Coupling this with an agile mindset that embraces change ensures they are not merely keeping up with the competition but consistently staying ahead. The competitive edge lies in the ability to be strategic, flexible, and relentlessly focused on delivering value to customers. In a world where the market never stands still, success is found in forward-thinking leadership that seizes opportunities before they become industry standards.

CHAPTER 8

The Future of Sales Leadership

"Technology is best when it brings people together."

— **Matt Mullenweg**

As we look toward the future of sales leadership, it's clear that technology and ethics will play pivotal roles in shaping the landscape. Emerging technologies like machine learning and blockchain are redefining how businesses manage their sales processes, streamline operations, and build customer relationships. However, with this technological evolution comes a shift in what customers expect from the companies they engage with. Modern consumers seek more than just a product or service; they look for authenticity, transparency, and a commitment to values that resonate with their own.

In this chapter, we'll explore how sales leaders can harness the power of advanced technologies to optimize their strategies while balancing the growing demand for ethical selling practices. From leveraging data-driven insights to adopting corporate social responsibility (CSR) initiatives, successful sales leadership in the coming years will require a blend of innovation and integrity. We'll dive into strategies for building future-ready sales teams capable of navigating both digital transformation and the rising call for purpose-driven business practices. The future of sales isn't just about closing deals; it's about building trust, embracing innovation, and leading with purpose.

Emerging Technologies and Their Impact on Sales Leadership

In the rapidly changing world of sales, adopting new technologies has shifted from a luxury to a necessity. Innovations like machine learning, blockchain, and artificial intelligence (AI) are revolutionizing how businesses build customer relationships, monitor sales performance, and deliver highly personalized experiences. These cutting-edge tools are reshaping the future of sales, offering leaders new ways to optimize processes and meet evolving customer expectations.

Machine Learning in Sales Leadership

Machine learning (ML) is fundamentally reshaping the role of sales leadership, offering unprecedented opportunities to harness vast datasets for more strategic, data-driven decision-making. As the adoption of ML technologies continues to grow, sales leaders must become adept at integrating these advanced tools to enhance productivity, strengthen customer relationships, and drive sustainable revenue growth. Understanding the potential of ML and how to apply it effectively can transform how sales teams operate, making them more agile, efficient, and customer-focused.

The Role of Machine Learning in Sales

Machine learning offers a powerful way to analyze customer data, revealing patterns that help predict buying behaviors, segment audiences more effectively, and identify winning sales strategies. This capability allows sales teams to make smarter, data-backed decisions, automate time-consuming tasks, and focus on the activities that truly matter, such as building meaningful relationships with clients and closing deals. Here's how ML is revolutionizing various aspects of the sales process:

- **Predictive Analytics:** One of the most impactful applications of ML in sales is predictive analytics. By analyzing historical data, market trends, and customer behaviors, ML can forecast future customer actions. This enables sales leaders to allocate resources more strategically, focusing efforts on high-potential markets or customer segments. For instance, an ML model might predict a surge in demand for a particular product category based on seasonal trends and past purchasing behaviors, allowing sales teams to adjust their approach accordingly. This proactive stance ensures that sales teams are not just reacting to market shifts but anticipating them, staying ahead of the curve[60].

- **Lead Scoring:** ML can dramatically improve the effectiveness of lead scoring, which is the process of ranking prospects based on their likelihood to convert. By analyzing past interactions, purchase patterns, and engagement metrics, ML models can identify which leads are most likely to become paying customers. This targeted approach allows sales professionals to focus their time and energy on the most promising prospects, significantly improving conversion rates. For example, a machine learning algorithm might prioritize a lead who has frequently visited a product page and engaged with marketing emails, signaling higher intent compared to a lead with minimal interaction.

- **Sales Process Automation:** Machine learning also plays a critical role in automating routine sales tasks, such as data entry, follow-up emails, and report generation. By automating these time-consuming activities, ML allows sales representatives to reclaim valuable hours in their day, enabling them to concentrate on more complex, high-value tasks like negotiation and customer relationship management. For instance, AI-powered chatbots can handle initial customer inquiries, freeing up sales reps to focus on deeper engagement with high-potential leads. This shift not only increases productivity but

[60] https://www.scratchpad.com/blog/sales-ai

also enhances the overall customer experience by providing faster, more consistent responses[61].

Practical Applications of Machine Learning in Sales

The benefits of machine learning can be seen across various industries, and its practical applications in sales are vast. Consider the example of an e-commerce business that uses ML to analyze customer purchase behaviors and browsing patterns. By leveraging this data, the business can send personalized product recommendations to individual customers, such as suggesting complementary items or highlighting popular products that align with their interests. This strategy not only boosts conversion rates but also enhances customer satisfaction by providing a tailored shopping experience that feels intuitive and relevant.

Another example involves using ML for customer retention. By analyzing customer support interactions and purchase history, businesses can identify signs of churn, such as a drop in engagement or a sudden increase in customer complaints. With this information, sales teams can proactively reach out to at-risk customers with personalized offers or support, turning potential losses into opportunities for deeper engagement.

How to Leverage Machine Learning in Your Sales Strategy

To successfully integrate machine learning into your sales strategy, it's important to approach the process with a clear plan. Here's an interactive template to guide you through implementing ML effectively:

1. **Identify Repetitive Tasks:** Start by assessing your current sales process and identifying tasks that could benefit from automation. This might include lead qualification, customer segmentation, data entry, or routine follow-up communications.

---

61 https://sales-mind.ai/blog/machine-learning-in-sales

Pinpointing these areas will help you focus your ML efforts where they can make the biggest impact.

2. **Research ML Tools:** Explore the wide range of machine learning solutions available, such as Salesforce Einstein, HubSpot's AI features, and other AI-powered CRM systems. Each of these tools offers different capabilities, from predictive analytics to natural language processing, that can be customized to meet your business needs. Look for solutions that integrate seamlessly with your existing systems to ensure a smooth transition[62].

3. **Implement a Pilot Program:** Rather than overhauling your entire sales process at once, start with a pilot project. Choose a specific area to test the effectiveness of ML, such as automating lead scoring or generating personalized email campaigns. Track key performance indicators (KPIs) like conversion rates, time saved, and customer feedback to gauge the impact of the pilot program.

4. **Analyze Results and Scale:** After running the pilot program, analyze the results to determine what worked and where there's room for improvement. Use the insights gained to refine your approach and gradually expand the use of ML across other aspects of your sales operations. This iterative approach ensures that you're making data-driven decisions at every step of the integration process[63].

---

[62] https://www.akkio.com/post/machine-learning-for-sales-a-practical-guide
[63] https://clickup.com/templates/project-plan/machine-learning

By following this structured approach, sales leaders can harness the full potential of machine learning, transforming their sales processes into a more efficient, customer-centric, and growth-oriented operation.

AI in Sales Leadership

Artificial Intelligence (AI) is reshaping the world of sales leadership, offering powerful tools to streamline processes, enhance customer engagement, and derive actionable insights from vast data sets. As organizations increasingly adopt AI technologies, sales leaders have a unique opportunity to leverage these advancements to optimize their strategies, boost productivity, and drive sustainable growth. Understanding how to harness the power of AI can position sales teams to thrive in a competitive market.

Key Benefits of AI in Sales

The integration of AI into sales processes offers a range of benefits that can significantly improve operational efficiency and the effectiveness of sales strategies. Here are some of the key advantages:

- **Enhanced Efficiency:** AI excels at automating repetitive and time-consuming tasks such as data entry, appointment scheduling, and follow-up reminders. This automation allows sales representatives to focus on higher-value activities, like building relationships and strategic planning. For example, AI can automatically schedule meetings based on customer availability, eliminating the back-and-forth of coordinating schedules. This increased efficiency not only shortens the sales cycle but also empowers sales teams to manage a larger volume of leads without compromising quality[64].

---

[64]https://www.xcellimark.com/blog/benefits-of-artificial-intelligence-ai-for-sales

- **Improved Accuracy:** One of the standout features of AI is its ability to analyze data with a level of precision that reduces human error. Advanced AI algorithms can process large volumes of data, leading to more accurate forecasting, reporting, and performance analysis. This accuracy is particularly valuable in sales forecasting, where even a small error can lead to missed opportunities or misallocated resources. By providing reliable data, AI enables sales leaders to make informed decisions that align with real market conditions, enhancing the overall effectiveness of sales planning and execution.

- **Real-Time Insights:** AI's ability to process and analyze data in real-time offers a significant competitive advantage. Sales teams can gain immediate insights into customer behavior, market trends, and sales performance, allowing them to make swift adjustments to their strategies. For instance, AI can monitor changes in customer purchase patterns and suggest adjustments to sales pitches or promotions on the fly. This agility enables sales teams to stay responsive to evolving customer needs and maintain a competitive edge in fast-moving markets.

- **Cost Reduction:** By automating routine tasks and optimizing sales processes, AI can significantly reduce operational costs. Automation minimizes the need for manual intervention in tasks like data processing, lead scoring, and report generation. Additionally, AI-driven tools can help allocate resources more effectively, ensuring that the sales team's efforts are concentrated on high-potential opportunities. This efficient use of resources leads to a better return on investment (ROI) for sales activities, allowing businesses to scale their efforts without proportionately increasing costs.

Transforming Sales Processes with AI

AI's influence spans various stages of the sales process, offering innovative solutions to common challenges. Here's how AI is revolutionizing key aspects of the sales journey:

- **Lead Generation:** AI-powered algorithms can analyze vast amounts of customer data to identify patterns and trends, helping sales teams pinpoint high-potential leads. By analyzing factors like purchase history, browsing behavior, and social media engagement, AI can predict which leads are most likely to convert. This targeted approach saves time and resources by allowing sales teams to focus on the most promising prospects rather than relying on traditional methods like cold calling or generic outreach. For example, an AI tool can prioritize leads based on their engagement with marketing emails, directing sales reps to those who are most interested in the product.

- **Sales Forecasting:** AI can utilize historical sales data, market trends, and customer behavior patterns to predict future sales outcomes with a high degree of accuracy. This predictive capability aids in better resource allocation and strategic planning, ensuring that sales teams are well-prepared for shifts in demand. For instance, a retail business could use AI to anticipate a spike in demand for certain products during the holiday season, allowing it to adjust inventory and staffing accordingly. This foresight not only improves preparedness but also helps businesses optimize their sales efforts to meet future market conditions.

- **Sales Pipeline Management:** Managing a sales pipeline effectively is crucial for converting leads into customers. AI enhances pipeline management by providing real-time insights into each stage of the sales funnel. This visibility allows sales leaders to identify potential bottlenecks, prioritize deals that are most likely to close, and ensure that opportunities move smoothly through the pipeline. For example, AI tools can analyze the length of time deals spend at each stage and suggest actions to accelerate the process, such as sending follow-up emails or scheduling calls at optimal times.

- **Dynamic Pricing Strategies:** AI can analyze market demand, competitor pricing, and customer profiles to implement dynamic pricing models that maximize profitability. By adjusting prices based on real-time conditions, such as inventory levels or seasonal trends, businesses can remain competitive while increasing sales. For instance, an AI-driven pricing engine could automatically offer discounts during slower sales periods to attract more customers and then adjust prices upward when demand peaks. This flexibility ensures that businesses can adapt to market conditions without sacrificing profitability[65].

Enhancing Customer Engagement with AI

AI's ability to process data and personalize interactions has made it an invaluable tool for enhancing customer engagement. By creating tailored experiences, AI helps build stronger relationships and increases customer satisfaction:

- **Personalized Recommendations:** AI can analyze a customer's past purchases, browsing behavior, and preferences to deliver personalized product recommendations. This tailored approach makes customers feel understood and valued, significantly increasing the likelihood of conversion. For example, an online retailer can use AI to suggest products that align with a customer's previous purchases, offering complementary items that enhance their shopping experience. This not only boosts sales but also enhances customer loyalty by providing a more relevant and engaging shopping journey[66].

---

[65] https://www.leewayhertz.com/ai-in-sales/
[66] https://www.nutshell.com/blog/ai-for-sales

- **Automated Communication:** AI-driven chatbots and virtual assistants can handle routine customer inquiries, providing instant responses and freeing up human agents to focus on more complex issues. These chatbots can assist with tasks such as answering common questions, processing orders, or scheduling appointments. By offering 24/7 support, AI enhances the customer experience, ensuring that clients receive timely assistance even outside of regular business hours. Moreover, AI-powered communication tools can analyze the tone and context of customer messages, enabling them to respond more effectively and empathetically, which further improves customer satisfaction[67].

Real-World Example- AI-Driven Transformation in Sales

Consider a mid-sized software company that implemented AI tools to enhance its sales process. By integrating an AI-powered CRM, the company was able to automate lead scoring and focus its efforts on high-value prospects. The AI system analyzed customer interactions and purchase history, prioritizing leads that had shown the most engagement. This allowed sales reps to concentrate their efforts on those leads, increasing conversion rates by 20%.

The company also used AI to optimize its email marketing campaigns, using machine learning algorithms to predict the best times to reach out to different customer segments. This adjustment led to a 15% increase in email open rates and a 10% boost in engagement with promotional content. By automating repetitive tasks and refining its approach to customer outreach, the company not only reduced its sales cycle but also enhanced customer relationships, demonstrating the transformative power of AI in modern sales.

---

67 https://improvado.io/blog/ai-sales-strategies

Blockchain in Sales Leadership

Blockchain technology is rapidly emerging as a game-changing tool in sales leadership, particularly for enhancing trust and transparency in customer relationship management (CRM) systems. Unlike traditional databases, which are often centralized and vulnerable to data manipulation, blockchain offers a secure, decentralized ledger that provides a permanent and transparent record of transactions. This capability makes blockchain particularly valuable for building trust between businesses and their customers, ensuring that interactions are authentic and that data remains secure. For sales leaders, integrating blockchain can transform how they manage customer relationships, authenticate products, and streamline sales processes.

Key Features of Blockchain in Sales

Blockchain's unique attributes make it an attractive solution for sales leaders seeking to improve transparency and data integrity. Here are the key features that set blockchain apart:

- **Decentralization:** Unlike conventional databases that are managed by a single entity, blockchain operates on a decentralized network of computers. Each participant in the network has access to a copy of the entire ledger, ensuring that no single party has undue control over the data. This decentralized structure reduces the risk of data manipulation or unauthorized access, as all participants have equal visibility into transactions. For sales leaders, this means greater security and transparency, making it easier to verify the authenticity of customer interactions and financial transactions without relying on a central authority.

- **Immutability:** One of the most powerful features of blockchain is its immutability. Once data is recorded on the blockchain, it cannot be altered or deleted, creating a permanent and tamper-proof record. This immutability ensures the integrity of transaction data and provides a reliable audit trail for sales transactions, customer records, and product information. For instance, if a customer disputes a transaction, sales leaders can refer to the immutable record on the blockchain, ensuring transparency and accountability.

- **Transparency:** Blockchain's transparency is another critical advantage for sales. Every transaction on the blockchain is recorded in a public or private ledger that is visible to all participants in the network. This transparency fosters trust between businesses and customers, as both parties can verify the authenticity of transactions without needing third-party verification. For sales teams, this means building stronger relationships with customers by offering clear and verifiable data about their interactions and purchases.

Enhancing Customer Trust Through Blockchain

In an era where customer trust is paramount, blockchain offers a unique opportunity to elevate transparency and credibility. Its application in sales can significantly enhance customer trust by ensuring the authenticity of products and the integrity of transactions:

- **Proof of Authenticity:** One of the most promising applications of blockchain in sales is providing proof of authenticity for products. For example, a company that sells luxury goods, such as watches or designer handbags, can use blockchain to record the entire history of each product, from manufacturing to final sale. By scanning a QR code or accessing the blockchain ledger, customers can verify the origin, authenticity, and ownership history of their purchase. This level of transparency not only reduces counterfeiting but also increases consumer confidence in the brand, as customers can trust that they are buying genuine products.

- **Secure Contracts:** Blockchain enables the creation of smart contracts, which are self-executing contracts with terms directly written into code on the blockchain. These contracts automatically trigger actions when predefined conditions are met, such as releasing payment when a product is delivered. Smart contracts eliminate the need for intermediaries, reducing the potential for human error or disputes. For sales leaders, this means faster, more secure transactions and a streamlined sales process that minimizes delays and enhances customer satisfaction.

Real-World Applications of Blockchain in Sales

Blockchain's potential is already being realized across various industries, with applications that demonstrate its ability to transform sales processes. Here are a few key examples:

- **Supply Chain Transparency:** In industries where supply chain integrity is critical, such as food, pharmaceuticals, and luxury goods, blockchain provides a way to track products from origin to delivery. For example, Walmart has implemented blockchain to monitor the journey of food products through its supply chain, allowing the company to trace items back to their source in a matter of seconds rather than weeks. This capability not only ensures the quality and safety of products but also boosts consumer trust by offering full transparency into the supply chain. For sales teams, this means the ability to guarantee product authenticity and safety, which can be a powerful selling point for quality-conscious customers.

- **Customer Data Management:** Managing customer data securely is a top priority for many industries, especially in finance, healthcare, and e-commerce. Blockchain offers a robust solution for securely storing and managing customer identities and transaction records. By using blockchain for identity verification, businesses can protect sensitive customer information from tampering and unauthorized access. This is particularly valuable in sectors where identity theft and data breaches are significant concerns. For sales leaders, adopting blockchain for customer data management not only ensures compliance with data protection regulations but also builds trust by demonstrating a commitment to safeguarding customer privacy.

- **Streamlined Loyalty Programs:** Blockchain can also revolutionize how companies manage customer loyalty programs. Traditionally, loyalty programs involve complex databases and multiple touchpoints, making them difficult to track and manage. With blockchain, businesses can create decentralized loyalty platforms where customers can earn, transfer, and redeem rewards with greater flexibility and transparency. This system simplifies the process, making it more convenient for customers while reducing administrative overhead for businesses. For sales teams, blockchain-enabled loyalty programs can boost customer retention and engagement, offering a seamless way for customers to interact with the brand.

Example- A Business Using Blockchain for Trust and Transparency

Consider a family-owned winery that has built its reputation on producing high-quality, organic wines. To further differentiate itself in a crowded market, the winery decides to use blockchain technology to verify the authenticity of its products. Each bottle of wine is tagged with a unique QR code that links to a blockchain ledger, documenting its journey from vineyard to shelf.

Customers can scan the code to access information about the grape variety, the vintage, the date of harvest, and even details about the winemaking process. This transparency not only appeals to the growing number of consumers who value traceability in their purchases but also positions the winery as a leader in quality and authenticity. As a result, the winery sees a boost in customer loyalty and attracts new clientele who value the assurance that they are getting exactly what they pay for.

This example illustrates how any business can leverage blockchain to build trust, differentiate themselves, and enhance their customer relationships.

Quick Poll: Are You Ready for Blockchain?

How familiar are you with blockchain technology and its sales applications?

☐ Not at all familiar

☐ Somewhat familiar

☐ Very familiar

Now that you've obtained deep insights into the emerging technologies in sales leadership, let's take a look at other key aspects:

The Growing Importance of Ethical Selling in Sales Leadership

In today's marketplace, ethical selling has evolved from a "nice-to-have" aspect to a core component of a company's identity. With consumers becoming more aware of social, environmental, and ethical issues, they increasingly seek out businesses that align with their values. This shift reflects a fundamental change in buyer behavior, one that prioritizes trust and integrity as much as the products or services being offered. For sales leaders, adopting ethical practices is no longer optional; it is a strategic imperative that can differentiate their brand in a competitive landscape. Ethical selling practices emphasize honesty, transparency, and fairness in every customer interaction, creating a foundation for long-term success.

The Essence of Ethical Selling

Ethical selling centers on the idea that sales should be about more than just hitting targets; it's about genuinely meeting the customer's needs. By placing the customer's interests above short-term sales goals, businesses can build lasting relationships grounded in trust and mutual respect. Here are the core elements that define ethical selling:

- **Honesty and Transparency:** Sales teams must provide clear, accurate, and truthful information about products and services. This means avoiding overpromising or making misleading claims about product capabilities. When customers have realistic expectations based on honest information, trust is built. For example, if a software solution has limitations, sales reps should communicate those openly, enabling customers to make well-informed decisions.

- **Fairness:** Ethical selling involves treating every customer with fairness and respect, ensuring that pricing is transparent and justifiable. It also means steering clear of high-pressure sales tactics that may coerce customers into decisions they aren't comfortable with. A fair approach respects the customer's autonomy, leading to more positive experiences and higher satisfaction levels.

- **Customer-Centric Focus:** An ethical sales strategy prioritizes understanding the customer's unique needs and offering solutions that genuinely address those needs. Rather than pushing products for the sake of making a sale, ethical sales professionals take the time to listen, understand, and recommend products or services that will provide real value to the customer.

By adhering to these principles, sales leaders can foster a culture where customer satisfaction is not just a goal but a core value that drives the entire sales process.

The Benefits of Ethical Selling

Adopting an ethical approach to sales brings a multitude of benefits that extend beyond immediate revenue. While the initial focus may be on building trust, the long-term rewards include stronger customer loyalty, a positive brand reputation, and sustainable growth:

- **Enhanced Customer Trust:** Trust is a cornerstone of successful sales relationships. Research by Integrity Solutions shows that organizations that prioritize ethical practices enjoy higher levels of customer loyalty and satisfaction. When customers perceive a brand as trustworthy, they are more likely to become repeat buyers and advocates, contributing to long-term revenue stability[68].

- **Positive Brand Reputation:** A reputation for ethical practices attracts positive attention not only from customers but also from industry peers and the media. This positive perception can lead to organic growth through word-of-mouth referrals and social media endorsements. In an era where customer reviews and social proof are critical to success, being known for ethical selling can be a powerful differentiator.

- **Long-Term Sustainability:** While unethical practices might yield short-term gains, they often come with long-term risks such as legal challenges, reputational damage, and high customer churn. Ethical businesses are better positioned for sustainable success because they build a loyal customer base that appreciates transparency and integrity. This foundation makes it easier to weather economic downturns and adapt to changing market conditions[69].

Principles of Ethical Selling

For sales leaders looking to embed ethical selling into their team's daily practices, it's important to follow a set of guiding principles. These principles ensure that every interaction with a customer aligns with the company's commitment to integrity:

1. **Ensure Product Fit:** Confirm that the product or service genuinely meets the customer's needs before closing a sale. This

---

[68] https://www.integritysolutions.com/blog/principles-ethical-sales-practices/

[69] https://www.kennect.io/post/sales-ethics

builds credibility and ensures that customers feel valued rather than just seen as a revenue source.

2. **Be Transparent:** Clearly communicate all pricing, terms, and conditions, avoiding hidden fees or ambiguous terms. Transparency helps to prevent misunderstandings and ensures that customers feel confident in their purchasing decisions.

3. **Avoid High-Pressure Tactics:** Foster an environment where customers feel comfortable making informed decisions. Sales should be about providing options and solutions, not applying undue pressure to close a deal.

4. **Treat Customers Fairly:** Ensure that every customer, regardless of their background or purchasing power, is treated with the same level of respect and fairness. This approach builds a more inclusive and welcoming brand image.

5. **Provide Accurate Information:** Always share truthful information about the benefits and limitations of your products or services. By being upfront about potential drawbacks, sales teams can manage expectations and build stronger, more trusting relationships[70].

Real-World Example- Ethical Selling in Action

Consider a renewable energy company that prides itself on transparency and customer education. Rather than pushing potential clients into purchasing solar panels, their sales team takes the time to assess each household's energy needs, financial situation, and long-term goals. They provide a detailed analysis of expected savings, potential drawbacks, and realistic timelines for return on investment. This upfront honesty, even when it means turning down clients who

---

[70] https://sales4good.org/the-7-guidelines-of-ethical-selling/?lang=en

wouldn't benefit from their products, has earned the company a strong reputation for integrity.

As a result, the company sees high levels of customer referrals and enjoys a loyal customer base that values its commitment to transparency. This approach demonstrates that ethical selling is not just about doing the right thing—it's also a smart business strategy that builds trust and drives long-term success.

The Growing Importance of Corporate Social Responsibility (CSR) in Sales Leadership

Corporate Social Responsibility (CSR) has evolved from being a peripheral consideration to a core component of business strategy in today's marketplace. As consumers, especially millennials and Gen Z, increasingly prioritize ethical and sustainable practices in their purchasing decisions, the role of CSR in shaping a company's brand identity and sales approach has never been more critical. This trend underscores a broader societal expectation: businesses should strive to contribute positively to society and the environment, going beyond the traditional pursuit of profits. For sales leaders, integrating CSR into their strategies is essential not only for appealing to modern buyers but also for positioning their companies as industry leaders in the years to come.

The Role of CSR in Modern Business

CSR encompasses a company's voluntary commitment to ethical business practices, environmental sustainability, fair labor standards, and community involvement. While adhering to legal standards is foundational, CSR takes this further by aiming to make a proactive, positive impact on society and the environment. This commitment might involve reducing carbon footprints, ensuring ethical supply chain practices, supporting local communities, or implementing diversity and inclusion initiatives.

Vision- Building a Future-Ready Sales Strategy with CSR

A forward-thinking sales strategy must be rooted in ethical values and sustainability goals that resonate with today's socially conscious consumers. By embedding CSR into their core business practices, sales leaders can strengthen their market position and cultivate deeper connections with customers. This alignment goes beyond short-term gains, creating a brand story that consumers are proud to support and share with others.

- **Consumer Expectations:** Modern consumers are increasingly likely to support brands that demonstrate a genuine commitment to social and environmental responsibility. According to a report by SurveySensum, CSR initiatives significantly boost brand image and customer loyalty, as consumers are drawn to companies that reflect their values. For example, customers are more inclined to buy from a brand that supports reforestation efforts or actively works to reduce plastic waste. Sales teams that effectively communicate these commitments can tap into a growing base of loyal customers[71].

- **Long-Term Success:** Emphasizing CSR is not just about meeting current trends; it's about building a resilient and adaptable business. Companies that adopt sustainable practices often discover new revenue streams, such as eco-friendly products, while simultaneously reducing operational costs linked to waste, energy consumption, and inefficiencies. For instance, a company that invests in energy-efficient technologies may not only cut utility costs but also attract customers who prioritize sustainability in their purchasing decisions. By making CSR a cornerstone of their sales strategy, businesses

---

[71] https://www.surveysensum.com/blog/csr-impact-customer-loyalty

can drive both economic and social value, ensuring sustainable growth in a competitive marketplace.

Interactive Checklist- Integrating CSR into Your Sales Strategy

Effectively incorporating CSR into a sales strategy requires a structured approach. Below is a checklist that sales leaders can use to align their operations with social responsibility:

Evaluate Your Current Practices:

☐ **Are your products/services sustainably sourced or produced?** Review your supply chain to ensure that the materials used align with environmental standards and ethical sourcing practices.

☐ **Does your business have fair labor policies in place?** Ensure that your company upholds fair wages and working conditions throughout your supply chain, whether in local or international operations.

☐ **Are you actively reducing your company's carbon footprint?** Implement measures such as energy-efficient practices, waste reduction, and carbon offset programs.

Align Sales Messaging with CSR:

☐ **Does your sales team understand and communicate your company's CSR initiatives?** Train sales teams to effectively articulate how the company's social and environmental efforts benefit customers and the broader community.

☐ **Are you highlighting the social or environmental benefits of your offerings in sales pitches?** Focus on how your product or service contributes to sustainability, such as reduced environmental impact or support for community programs.

Develop a CSR Action Plan:

☐ **Set clear, measurable CSR goals (e.g., reduce plastic waste by 20% within a year).** Establish specific targets that guide your sustainability efforts and provide a benchmark for success.

☐ **Incorporate sustainability into your product development and customer engagement strategies.** Consider designing new products with eco-friendly materials or offering discounts for customers who engage in recycling programs.

☐ **Share your progress with customers through newsletters, social media, or annual reports.** Transparency in sharing achievements and challenges builds trust and reinforces your commitment to continuous improvement.

Example- The Rise of Ethical Consumerism

Take the example of a skincare company that recognized a growing consumer demand for ethical and sustainable products. By reformulating its offerings to include only all-natural, cruelty-free ingredients and ensuring fair trade practices throughout its supply chain, the company aligned itself with the values of modern consumers. The sales team played a crucial role in this transformation by emphasizing transparency about ingredient sourcing and the company's commitment to environmental sustainability during sales conversations and marketing campaigns.

This approach not only differentiated the brand from larger, less transparent competitors but also resonated deeply with a new wave of ethically-minded consumers. As a result, the company saw a 35% increase in customer loyalty and a significant boost in word-of-mouth referrals, proving that aligning sales strategies with CSR can be a powerful driver of growth and brand advocacy.

Developing a Future-Ready Sales Strategy

In the evolving world of sales, success hinges on the ability to adapt and innovate. To stay ahead, sales leaders must design strategies that not only leverage technological advancements but also integrate ethical considerations. A future-ready sales strategy strikes a balance between using cutting-edge tools and maintaining a strong commitment to values that resonate with today's consumers. Here's how to build a strategy that prepares your sales team for long-term success:

Future-Ready Sales Strategy Framework

Component	Action	Reason
Technology Integration	Leverage AI, machine learning, and blockchain to automate sales processes and ensure transparency.	This approach boosts operational efficiency and builds trust by offering greater transparency in transactions. It allows sales teams to automate routine tasks, freeing up time for more strategic activities like relationship-building.
Customer-Centric Focus	Use data analytics to deliver personalized, relevant, and meaningful interactions with customers.	Personalization leads to higher customer engagement, satisfaction, and loyalty by addressing their unique needs and preferences. It turns data insights into targeted actions, such as tailored product recommendations and customized marketing messages.
Ethical Selling Practices	Implement fair, transparent, and honest sales approaches. Train sales teams to prioritize customer needs over aggressive sales tactics.	Ethical selling practices foster trust, making customers more likely to stay loyal and become brand advocates. It creates a culture of integrity that attracts repeat business and referrals, building a strong foundation for growth.

Corporate Social Responsibility (CSR)	Align your sales strategy with the company's commitment to social, ethical, and environmental responsibilities. Showcase these efforts in sales interactions.	Today's consumers increasingly choose brands that align with their values. Integrating CSR into sales messaging not only attracts socially conscious buyers but also strengthens the company's overall brand reputation, making it a preferred choice in a competitive market.
Agility and Innovation	Foster a mindset of continuous improvement by testing new technologies, approaches, and strategies. Encourage a culture of flexibility within the sales team.	In a rapidly changing market, agility is key. Being willing to experiment with new tools and adapt to shifting consumer behaviors allows the sales team to respond swiftly to new opportunities and challenges, maintaining a competitive edge.

CHAPTER 9

Embracing Change and Using Stress to Promote Growth

In today's fast-paced and ever-evolving business environment, change is not just an occasional disruption; it's the foundation of growth and resilience. Companies and individuals who excel in this landscape have learned to embrace change as an essential aspect of their journey. However, with change often comes stress, a natural, even protective response that can feel overwhelming if not managed correctly. Instead of viewing stress as an obstacle, this chapter explores the potential of stress as a catalyst for growth, creativity, and resilience.

By reframing stress and equipping teams with strategies to adapt, leaders can transform the experience of change into an empowering journey. This chapter dives into understanding stress as an asset, offering insights into building an adaptable mindset and creating a resilient team culture that thrives amid change. By harnessing stress and viewing change as an opportunity, leaders and teams can develop the strength to turn uncertainty into innovation and anxiety into productivity.

Understanding the Role of Change in Growth

The business landscape is driven by constant evolution, from shifting technologies to rising customer expectations. In this world of relentless innovation, success hinges on the ability to proactively embrace change as an opportunity for growth rather than viewing it as a disruption to the status quo. Companies that cultivate a change-ready culture remain agile, prepared to meet market demands, and equipped to seize emerging opportunities with confidence.

For individuals and teams, embracing change opens doors to new skill sets, mindsets, and challenges that foster growth and development. When change is normalized within a culture, teams become accustomed to adapting, learning, and improving, thereby fostering resilience as an organizational strength. Growth-oriented companies encourage employees to see change as a pathway to professional and personal development, enabling them to evolve alongside the organization.

Creating a Vision for Change: Leaders play a critical role in shaping a positive perspective on change by articulating a compelling vision that aligns with team values and goals. A clear, purpose-driven vision reassures team members that change serves a greater objective, transforming it from a disruptive force into a unifying mission.

Example: Consider a retail company transitioning to an e-commerce model in response to changing consumer preferences. By clearly outlining how this digital shift supports long-term growth and providing tailored training on digital tools, leaders transform an intimidating shift into an exciting, purpose-driven opportunity for growth. When teams see change as a way to contribute to the company's vision, they are more likely to embrace it with enthusiasm.

The Biological Basis and Transformative Potential of Stress

Stress is deeply rooted in our biology as a survival mechanism. When faced with change, our bodies release adrenaline and cortisol, which are hormones designed to help us respond quickly and with heightened focus. In short bursts, this stress response can be invaluable, providing the mental clarity and energy needed to tackle complex challenges. However, the modern workplace often triggers chronic stress, which, if unmanaged, can lead to burnout, fatigue, and diminished productivity.

Rather than viewing stress as an inevitable negative, understanding its biological purpose can help individuals and teams harness its potential. With the right mindset, stress can be reframed as an indication of growth, a sign that new skills and strategies are needed. Leaders can help their teams channel stress positively, using it as motivation to overcome obstacles and adapt to change.

Reframing Stress: Research suggests that viewing stress as a positive force can improve resilience, creativity, and problem-solving skills. By shifting from seeing stress as a burden to recognizing it as a motivator for growth, teams can approach challenges with renewed energy and optimism. When stress is perceived as a stepping stone rather than a setback, it fuels personal and professional growth.

Turning Stress into Motivation: Leaders can foster a growth mindset by encouraging teams to view stress as a sign of impending growth and innovation. By acknowledging stress as a natural reaction to the unknown, leaders empower their teams to use it as a source of focus and determination. When stress is embraced rather than resisted, it becomes a powerful tool for progress.

Case Study: Consider a software company undergoing a significant restructuring process. Initially, employees felt apprehensive and stressed about shifting roles and responsibilities. Recognizing this, the leadership introduced professional development programs aligned with the new structure, reframing the transition as an opportunity for skill-building. By encouraging employees to view stress as a prompt for growth, they transformed anxiety into engagement, and morale and productivity saw a substantial boost.

Identifying and Acknowledging Resistance to Change

Change in any organization can stir up resistance, a natural response rooted in the fear of the unknown or the perceived loss of stability. Resistance may arise from diverse sources, such as concerns about increased workload, anxiety over job security, or doubts about adapting to new expectations. Leaders play an essential role in recognizing these concerns and addressing them proactively, setting the stage for a smoother transition and fostering a culture of openness and resilience.

Recognizing Root Causes of Resistance

The first step in overcoming resistance is identifying its underlying causes. Recognizing the specific concerns that individuals or teams have about change allows leaders to provide targeted support and alleviate fears. Leaders can gain valuable insights through various methods, such as team surveys, one-on-one conversations, and anonymous feedback channels. These tools help uncover the reasons behind resistance, whether it's fear of additional workload or uncertainty about adapting to new tools.

Example: Suppose a team resists the introduction of new project management software, fearing that it will increase their workload. By directly addressing these concerns, perhaps by discussing options for redistributing tasks or clarifying how the tool will streamline processes, leaders can help ease the transition and demonstrate a commitment to their team's well-being.

Suggested Activity: Conduct a team-wide survey or individual interviews to gather insights into specific concerns related to upcoming changes. Use the information gathered to create solutions that directly address these areas, helping to ease the transition and minimize resistance.

Providing Validation and Empathy

Acknowledging and validating team members' feelings about change helps to create an environment of trust and openness. When leaders listen and empathize, employees feel that their concerns are respected. This validation fosters a sense of psychological safety, where employees are more willing to share concerns, ask questions, and ultimately engage in the change process.

By recognizing resistance as a natural reaction rather than an obstacle, leaders create a supportive atmosphere where open dialogue is encouraged. When team members feel heard, they're more likely to shift from a place of apprehension to one of acceptance and even enthusiasm.

Communicating the Benefits of Change Clearly

One of the most effective ways to secure team buy-in is to communicate the rationale behind the change clearly. When team members understand how change aligns with their own goals and see the benefits it can bring, they are much more likely to embrace it. Leaders who communicate openly about the advantages of change foster a sense of shared purpose, reduce anxiety, and enable teams to see how the change will directly enhance their daily workflows or create new opportunities.

Aligning Change with Team Goals: For change to be meaningful, it should connect with the personal and professional aspirations of team members. For instance, if a new Customer Relationship Management (CRM) tool is being introduced, explaining how it will streamline tasks and reduce repetitive work can help team members understand its benefits. When individuals can see how a change enhances their roles, it feels less like an imposed adjustment and more like a path toward growth.

Outlining Short- and Long-Term Benefits: Discussing both the immediate and long-term benefits of change helps team members understand the full scope of value. Short-term wins, such as reduced workload or increased efficiency, provide quick validation, while long-term outcomes, like skill development or career growth, create motivation and reinforce the advantages of the change.

Suggested Activity: Host a team meeting specifically to outline the benefits of the change. After the presentation, open the floor to a Q&A session, where team members can ask questions or express any concerns. This open discussion helps clarify misunderstandings, ensuring that everyone is aligned on how the change can positively impact their roles.

Involving the Team in the Change Process

Involving team members in the change process significantly reduces resistance and builds enthusiasm. When individuals have a voice in how change is implemented, they feel a sense of ownership and are more committed to its success. Collaborative involvement not only makes the transition smoother but also fosters a more inclusive culture.

Encouraging Feedback and Ideas: Actively inviting team members to provide feedback or suggest ideas demonstrates that their input is valued and considered. Leaders who foster this engagement create a sense of trust and respect within the team. When people feel involved in shaping the change, they're more likely to approach it with an open mind and a willingness to contribute to its success.

Building a Collaborative Culture: By involving team members in planning and decision-making, leaders promote a culture of collaboration. A participative approach helps ensure that change aligns with team needs, fostering a supportive environment where employees feel that their perspectives matter. This approach not only smooths the transition but also enhances team morale and unity.

Example: A healthcare company implementing a new scheduling system invited representatives from each department to form a "change committee." This group was responsible for gathering feedback, testing the system, and recommending improvements. By involving team members in the process, the company fostered a sense of ownership and eased the transition.

Suggested Activity: Establish a "change committee" with representatives from various roles within the team. This group can be involved in pilot testing, sharing ideas, and providing feedback, helping to shape the change in ways that resonate with team members.

Providing Training and Resources to Support Change

Change often involves adopting new tools, systems, or roles, which can feel daunting if employees are not adequately prepared. Comprehensive training and resources help team members adapt effectively, reducing uncertainty and boosting confidence. When individuals feel equipped and supported, they are far more likely to view change as an opportunity for growth rather than a disruption to their routine.

Offering Tailored Training: Providing customized training sessions that address specific needs, whether through hands-on workshops, online modules, or one-on-one coaching, can build team members' competence and confidence in adapting to new tasks or technologies. Tailored training demonstrates that leaders are invested in the growth and development of their team, helping employees feel more comfortable and capable in their roles.

Creating a Resource Hub: Establishing a centralized hub containing tutorials, FAQs, and other reference materials provides a go-to resource for team members as they navigate new systems. This accessible resource center empowers employees to troubleshoot issues independently, ensuring a smoother, more confident transition.

Example: A financial services company implementing a new CRM created a comprehensive training program that included tutorials, hands-on workshops, and an online knowledge hub. Team members were encouraged to ask questions and offer feedback, resulting in a more engaged team and a seamless transition.

Suggested Activity: Organize a series of workshops or training sessions tailored to the skills required by the new changes. These sessions not only build confidence but also reassure team members that they have the support needed to succeed.

Celebrating Milestones and Small Wins

Recognizing and celebrating progress, even the smallest achievements, plays a crucial role in sustaining team morale and motivation. During periods of change, acknowledging these "small wins" reminds team members that their hard work is making a difference, fostering a positive environment and encouraging continued engagement.

Creating Meaningful Recognition Moments

Leaders should prioritize making recognition moments meaningful and tailored to the team's efforts and culture. Celebrations, whether they're grand or subtle, reinforce a sense of accomplishment and validate the commitment of each team member. Rather than simply acknowledging a job done, meaningful recognition connects the team's achievements to the organization's broader goals, making everyone feel valued and integral to the success story.

Example: If a team reaches a significant milestone, such as completing a phase of a new project implementation, a leader might celebrate by organizing a team lunch, presenting personalized recognition notes, or sharing a congratulatory post on the company's internal platform. These gestures reinforce the message that individual and collective contributions are appreciated and vital to the organization.

Setting Milestone Goals for Consistent Progress

Breaking larger projects into smaller, more achievable goals helps teams maintain a sense of progress and reduces the feeling of being overwhelmed. Milestones create touchpoints where success can be measured, motivating the team to keep moving forward. Celebrating each milestone doesn't just boost morale but also provides a regular reminder of how much has been accomplished, validating the team's efforts and fostering a positive outlook on the change.

Suggested Activity: Create a visual milestone tracker, such as a progress board or digital dashboard, that highlights completed stages and upcoming targets. Update it regularly and celebrate each milestone with a quick team huddle, a shout-out, or even an impromptu snack break. This visual reinforcement cultivates a sense of ongoing achievement and keeps the team motivated.

Providing Ongoing Support and Reinforcement

Transitioning to new systems, processes, or ways of working doesn't happen overnight. Teams need consistent support and reinforcement to prevent backsliding into old habits, which can undermine the progress made. Ongoing support, check-ins, and access to resources demonstrate the organization's commitment to helping the team navigate the change successfully.

Establishing Regular Check-Ins

Regular check-ins offer an opportunity for leaders to assess the team's progress, address any ongoing challenges, and provide guidance as needed. These sessions not only reinforce the importance of the change but also create a feedback loop where employees feel comfortable sharing their experiences, asking questions, and receiving personalized support.

Example: Leaders at a company introducing a new project management tool might hold weekly check-ins where team members can discuss challenges, share progress, and receive tips on maximizing the tool's effectiveness. This steady flow of communication makes the transition smoother and empowers the team to voice concerns and celebrate small successes along the way.

Creating a Support Network for Adaptability

A support network, whether through mentorship, peer support, or a buddy system, offers team members a reliable source of encouragement and guidance. This network allows individuals to share experiences, troubleshoot issues collaboratively, and reinforce each other's adaptability. A buddy system, for example, pairs team members to provide mutual support and accountability, creating a more connected, supportive work environment.

Suggested Activity: Establish a buddy system or change support group where team members pair up for guidance and motivation. By sharing their journeys, they can manage stress constructively, exchange insights, and celebrate individual and team achievements together.

Transforming Stress into a Catalyst for Growth

Stress often accompanies change, but when managed constructively, it can fuel innovation, strengthen focus, and enhance team cohesion. Leaders can guide their teams in harnessing stress as a force for positive transformation by fostering resilience, adaptability, and a growth-oriented mindset.

Using Stress as a Springboard for Innovation

Stress often signals that something new is required, prompting individuals and teams to think creatively and solve problems with fresh approaches. Encouraging a mindset that views stress as a trigger for innovation rather than a barrier can lead to breakthrough ideas and improved processes. By reframing stress as a prompt for constructive action, leaders can help their teams channel this energy into finding innovative solutions.

Building Focus and Resilience Amid Pressure

Stress heightens focus and urgency, which can be powerful when channeled effectively. By fostering a team culture that emphasizes resilience and adaptability, leaders can help their teams develop the mental toughness needed to meet goals, even in high-pressure situations. When stress is viewed as a motivator, it enhances productivity and inspires teams to push through challenges with determination.

Strengthening Team Bonds Through Shared Challenges

Facing stress as a collective fosters stronger team bonds. When teams work through challenging situations together, they build trust, empathy, and camaraderie. Leaders who encourage open communication, mutual support, and shared problem-solving create a collaborative environment that endures under pressure, fostering loyalty and a shared commitment to success.

Suggested Exercises: Host a workshop on positive stress management techniques, encouraging team members to reframe stress as a natural component of growth. Provide mindfulness exercises and time-management strategies to equip employees with practical tools for handling stress effectively.

The Path Forward- A Culture of Adaptability and Success

In a constantly changing world, organizations that embrace stress as a catalyst for growth and adaptability are better positioned to thrive. When change is supported by open communication, consistent recognition, and ongoing reinforcement, it transforms from a source of anxiety into an empowering opportunity for development and innovation.

By cultivating a culture that sees stress as an ally and change as a springboard for success, leaders build a resilient, future-ready organization. The journey of adaptation becomes a shared mission, one in which each team member feels empowered to grow, innovate, and contribute to a vision of lasting success.

www.ingramcontent.com/pod-product-compliance
Lightning Source LLC
LaVergne TN
LVHW022039200926
848481LV00003B/721
* 9 7 9 8 3 4 9 3 2 2 2 3 5 *